JUDO
UNLEASHED!

Neil Ohlenkamp

JUDO
UNLEASHED!

The Ultimate Training Bible
For Judoka at Every Level

TUTTLE Publishing

Tokyo | Rutland, Vermont | Singapore

CONTENTS

"Nothing under the sun is greater than education. By educating one person and sending him into the society of his generation, we make a contribution extending a hundred generations to come." – Jigoro Kano

This book is dedicated to all judo teachers who share their knowledge and love of judo with their students, specifically to Juergen Wahl Sensei (1935–2021), who was an example and guide to the author for half a century. His contribution lives on in this book.

How to Use this Book

This book is a manual presenting the main principles and techniques of Kodokan Judo. The Kodokan is the original school of judo in Tokyo, Japan, founded in 1882. The techniques in the standard syllabus of judo are included as a reference, but there are many variations of each technique. The photographs in this book demonstrate the basic positions of the techniques and some variations, but you are invited to attend judo classes frequently to discover the intricacies that lead to mastery.

Participating in a judo class with other students under the supervision of a qualified judo instructor is the only way to develop skill in judo. This book is intended to give readers a greater understanding of judo, and to be a study aid and reference for students on their journey. Be assured that there is much more to learning judo than what is included here.

Safety is the first responsibility of every judo student. To begin you will need a health evaluation, proper training facilities, mats designed for judo, expert supervision, and personal instruction by a qualified judo teacher. This book can be an invaluable supplement to judo instruction, but a novice should not expect to develop good techniques solely from reading a book or practicing without an instructor. Poor technique can result in serious injury.

Strict adherence to safety precautions is required. Any physical activity can lead to injuries, but judo is a martial art based on combat skills, so it includes techniques that may cause injury or death. Improperly applied or misused, the techniques described in this book are dangerous. You must learn and practice these skills in a well-designed course of personal instruction that considers the individual readiness of you and your partner for each technique.

Every effort has been made to ensure that this book is accurate. However, it does not include every aspect of judo that a student needs to be familiar with to practice safely. The author has no knowledge of you or your training partner's readiness, health, ability, practice methods, etc. and does not accept liability for any accident, inconvenience, injury, claim, or loss. The author accepts no responsibility or liability for injuries resulting from practicing judo.

The technique names, Japanese terminology and English translations used in these chapters are those used in the official Kodokan New Japanese-English Dictionary of Judo (Kodokan Judo Institute, 2000) and Kodokan Judo by Jigoro Kano (Kodansha International, 1994). These are the most widely accepted, but you may see other terms used in various judo schools around the world.

—Neil Ohlenkamp

JUDO
FUNDAMENTALS

CHAPTER 1:
LEARNING ABOUT JUDO

Skill in judo can only be attained on the mat, working with partners in an organized training program under the guidance of an expert judo instructor, or *sensei,* which literally means 'one who has gone before'. A *sensei* has been in your position and learned the lessons you seek. By providing a good example and demonstrating proper technique, a *sensei* helps you understand the techniques and acts as a model by which to gauge your own performance.

You also learn from everyone with whom you practice, so seek instruction from a wide variety of people. Do not limit your training opportunities by being selective. You will soon see that even the model technique performed by your *sensei* may be modified to take advantage of your own strengths or body type. Likewise, the technique may vary depending on your opponent's height, weight, movement or abilities. Knowing this, you should feel free to try different methods, but only after learning the basic principle of the technique and progressing well beyond the beginner stage.

This book provides a reference for all the standard techniques of Kodokan Judo, but also gives the reader new ideas for techniques, variations, and training methods you may not see in class. Like practicing with your *sensei*, it will expand your understanding of judo, expose you to fresh ideas, and reinforce the basic principles of judo.

It will supplement your hands-on training by helping you to visualize the techniques and understand the key points that make judo work with minimal effort. Soon, with sufficient practice, you will be applying judo techniques with ease.

Physical training is needed to give you a palpable understanding of judo principles, but these chapters aim to provide glimpses of the underlying theories that explain how the training works to improve your skill, and to explore larger fighting principles that can be learned in judo. These topics are seldom discussed in depth during class, but your performance will improve as you deepen your understanding. Recognizing the limitless nature of attacks, you would have to learn an infinite number of techniques to master every potential situation. If you strive to understand the principles behind the art of attack and defense, you should eventually learn to respond more intuitively and naturally even in new situations.

Another objective of this manual is to help you through rough spots in training by encouraging you to see the possibilities as you prepare for each new rank. It cannot replace self-discipline, but it can act as a reference to show you the light at the end of the tunnel. To earn a black belt, you must devote a considerable part of your life to judo so you should know that it is achievable. As you advance, you will see that your effort is worth it when you're able to get results against increasingly difficult opponents.

Evolution of judo

Judo means many things to different people. It is a sport, an art, a discipline, a recreational activity, a fitness program, a study of Japanese culture, a means of self-defense, and a way of life. It is both one of the world's most practiced martial arts and Olympic sports. Let's look at how judo got to be so popular.

CLASSICAL JUDO

Judo is a consolidation and refinement of the combat systems of older Japanese *jujutsu*, where mastery of the art was essential to a warrior's survival in battle. *Jujutsu* (sometimes spelled *jujitsu* or *jiu jitsu*) was practiced in Japan for centuries by the *samurai* warrior class. It included a wide variety of hand-to-hand combat techniques, mostly kept secret by various schools, or *ryu*, that specialized in different types of fighting techniques.

> "What western brain could have elaborated this strange teaching, never to oppose force to force, but only to direct and utilize the power of attack; to overthrow the enemy solely by his own strength, to vanquish him solely by his own effort? Surely none!"
>
> *Out of the East: Reveries and Studies in New Japan* by Lafcadio Hearn, 1897.

Jigoro Kano, the founder of judo, was born in 1860 and studied traditional styles of *jujutsu* during his youth, a period when the practice of martial arts in Japan was dying out. While mastering the *Kito Ryu* and *Tenjin-shinyo Ryu* styles of *jujutsu* he often was the only student due to its lack of popularity, so he became devoted to teaching and preserving the older ways of fighting. He sought to retain much of the traditional Japanese culture and fighting methods in judo, partly by emphasizing the value of the continued practice of dangerous combat techniques, including various strikes to sensitive areas and defenses against weapons.

For this he promoted the use of a rehearsed training method called *kata*. He recognized that certain techniques and practice methods were in danger of disappearing because changing times meant they were no longer needed by the warrior class. By updating the practice of judo to make it more safe, effective and relevant for modern society, he saved much of the ancient warriors' knowledge and passed it on to new generations.

Jigoro Kano was both a traditionalist and an innovator. Although concerned about the loss of tradition during Japan's modernization, he embraced many changes. In 1882 he founded the Kodokan as the original school of judo – the first Japanese martial art of the modern era. It successfully preserved the techniques and spirit of *jujutsu* while at the same time breaking away from some of its traditional practice methods so that judo would conform to modern principles of physical education. Changes were made to ensure participants' safety, improve effectiveness and emphasize certain overall principles.

The refinements began by identifying the most dangerous moves of judo, and restricting these to *kata* practice. This permitted Jigoro Kano to improve on *jujutsu* training methods by focusing on the use of real-life free practice, or *randori*, with techniques that could be applied safely with full force against an opponent. It was a major advance in martial arts training, greatly improving the effectiveness of judo compared to earlier martial arts.

The development of *randori* as a form of practice led to a safe way to test and improve physical skills and combat spirit via competition, or *shiai*. Jigoro Kano created the first annual Red and White Tournament at the Kodokan in 1884. This competition continues today as one of the longest-running sporting events in the world, predating the modern Olympics by 12 years. In 1930 the Kodokan also began the annual All Japan Judo Championships. As other modern sports began to form and judo was introduced into the public school system, judo gradually developed a competitive element that helped to popularize it

Which is the best martial art? The one you will enjoy practising for the rest of your life.

The many facets of Judo

Judo is more about self-discovery than memorization of moves. Like a fine diamond, it has many facets reflecting the light of the world around it; each time you look at judo another reveals its brilliance.

- Judo can be applied without injuring an opponent, but it has also saved the lives of many students faced with real attacks.
- Judo has consistently proven its effectiveness in a wide range of tests from ancient *jujutsu* contests to modern mixed martial arts matches.
- Judo is included in military hand-to-hand combat training to efficiently apply force in a deadly manner.
- Judo competition is enjoyed by young children at local tournaments, and by elite male and female athletes who represent their countries at the Olympic Games, performing awesome feats of skill.

- Judo principles are studied in the best business schools around the world to help corporate leaders use power properly, utilize leverage and apply it in the right direction, as well as take advantage of competitors' greater strength and size by using it against them.
- Verbal judo is taught in many law enforcement agencies to provide officers with methods to de-escalate and control dangerous situations without using force.
- Judo is based on sound principles that help students develop character and become experts at dealing with all kinds of conflicts in life.

as a physical education system for the masses around the world.

As principal of the first teachers' training university in Tokyo, Jigoro Kano led Japan through great educational reform, and was the first Japanese delegate to the International Olympic Committee. Considered the father of sport in Japan, he oversaw and encouraged significant evolution of judo during his lifetime. Sometimes called *Kano-ryu jujutsu* early on, judo eventually overshadowed *jujutsu*, which all but disappeared for nearly 100 years as many of its styles merged into Kodokan Judo. Much of judo's popularity in Japan was a result of proven success in competitions, such as the great tournament of 1886 where the Kodokan defeated the feared *jujutsu* masters of the Meiji era.

Based on experience in competition, judo continued to change and adapt its techniques, as it does today. One famous tournament against *Fusen-ryu jujutsu* masters around the turn of the 20th century revealed a weakness in the judo syllabus and resulted in strengthening judo mat work (*newaza*) by incorporating some *Fusen-ryu* techniques and training methods. Further development of *newaza* came over 100 years ago as a result of training for *Kosen* judo competition in certain educational institutions, and more recently from the influence of Brazilian Jiu Jitsu, a popular offshoot specializing in *newaza*.

Jigoro Kano was always looking for ways to improve the performance of judo students in

contest. Based on tournament results, some techniques were banned because they were too dangerous, while new techniques were adopted once they proved effective. He recognized it was not only the type of techniques that determined the success or failure of a competitor or fighter; by focusing on training methods, he revolutionized the classical *jujutsu* approach to training. Counterintuitive as it seems, by separating the most dangerous techniques from free practice, he created a training method that actually permitted students to become more dangerous as fighters. Martial artists soon discovered that only by regular *randori* and *shiai* against fully resisting opponents did they gain the necessary skills to apply the techniques in a real situation – something not possible by practicing lightly against cooperating partners. Jigoro Kano realized that the most successful training results in body and mind working together instinctively to respond to unique situations with accuracy and confidence, rather than with theoretical, predetermined or tentative actions.

EVOLUTION OF SPORT JUDO

Judo is the first Olympic sport to have originated in Asia, with Jigoro Kano being the first Asian member of the International Olympic Committee. Judo was scheduled to be a demonstration sport in the 1940 Olympic Games to be held in Tokyo, Japan, but these Games were cancelled. After Jigoro Kano's death in 1938 – followed closely by World War II, the occupation of Japan and the westernization of Japanese culture – judo went through a period of turmoil. Eventually it transformed as the sporting aspects were emphasized and the historical combative nature was downplayed.

The formation of the International Judo Federation in 1951 and the introduction of judo into the modern Olympic Games in 1964 were big steps in its growth. The first Olympic Judo competition took place at the newly built Budokan in Tokyo, Japan, with 72 athletes participating from 27 countries. By the 2020 Olympic Games, again held at the Budokan in Tokyo, participation increased to 393 athletes from 126 countries. Medals were earned by 26 countries, compared to 8 countries that earned medals in the first Olympic judo competition.

The internationalization of competition dramatically influenced the course of judo development. Different countries adopted different training approaches with varying degrees of success. Modern research and sports training principles were incorporated into judo training.

Judo techniques and tactics changed as the rules evolved. As more people practiced judo, the level of competition increased, and contest effectiveness emerged as the ultimate measure of success.

According to the International Judo Federation (IJF), the world governing body for international judo competition, judo is undoubtedly the most popular combat sport and martial art in the world. There are 206 National Olympic Committees globally, and 200 have affiliated National Judo Federations, making it one of the most widespread of Olympic sports. World Championship gold medals have been earned by more than 35 different countries, and expertise in judo today can be found almost anywhere in the world.

JUDO TODAY

The steady progress towards judo as a sport that was made under Jigoro Kano has continued in the years since the creation of the International Judo Federation. Many people now think of judo simply as a sport because it is included along with other major sports in Olympic competition. Although

While judo is clearly rooted in traditional arts of war studied by the samurai, it is practiced today as a fun sport by millions of adults and children around the world.

Judo self-defense training

Jigoro Kano applied modern sport methodology to traditional *jujutsu* and found that it produced a better combat art because it added realism to the training by permitting full resistance from your opponent. Just as non-contact self-defense training will not provide the benefits of full-contact judo, training solely for sports contests will not provide complete self-defense training. The rules of judo competition provide a safe and challenging learning environment, but they also limit certain techniques that can be used in a real fight. This is why judo includes a number of non-competitive components.

Jigoro Kano was eager to preserve traditional self-defense techniques that could not be used safely in competition, including punches, kicks, knee locks and other joint locks. These techniques, as well as modern ones like handgun defenses, are learned in *kata* practice.

Many people train in judo primarily for self-defense. In one online poll of more than 2,700 people, 24 per cent said their main interest in judo was competition, while another 23 per cent said self-defense. Recreation or fun was the main interest of 19 per cent of the respondents, followed by physical fitness, character development and other interests.

For those who have never used sport-training methods, or those who have never explored traditional *bujutsu* (martial arts) training, it is easy to discount the effectiveness of the other. But in judo we should continually seek opportunities to challenge ourselves by examining the weaknesses in our training and keeping our minds open to other methods. Competing against an opponent in a contest can be an effective method of training for self-defense, while practicing the *kata* helps to learn specific techniques adapted to self-defense situations in a controlled manner.

Despite its high profile as a sport, many people consider judo to be strictly a martial art, with an emphasis on self-defense. There is a broad resurgence in the practice of *kata* around the world. It provides an alternative way to progress in the study of judo so that there is something for every age and interest. Over time your interest in judo may change, often from competition in your youth to *kata* practice as you age.

many judo students around the world regularly practice various strikes, joint locks and weapon defenses that are not permitted in competition, the emphasis on sport judo for the last 60 to 70 years has downplayed the significance of the full range of judo self-defense techniques preserved in the *kata*. As a result, the value of judo as a form of self-defense is sometimes misunderstood and underestimated.

Although still heavily influenced by the ideals of its founder, judo around the world today is quite different from what it was during its origins in 19th-century Japan. With the ever-growing popularization of sports in society and the downplaying of non-competition judo techniques, the question for the 21st century is, "Are we fighting or playing?" Is a judo match, and by extension judo practice, a serious preparation for life and death combat, or is it a competitive sport, like table tennis, with extrinsic rewards such as fame, trophies, or rank? Can you receive the benefits of both types of judo practice?

Other martial artists occasionally use the term sport to refer to judo as a game with no usefulness, implying it is only for play and cannot be effective for self-defense, fighting or combat. Some martial artists even think the distinction between sport and martial art is that martial artists train for real life while sport judo athletes are bound by unrealistic and restrictive rules designed to ensure safety rather than fighting effectiveness.

In fact, the distinction is more complex and rather surprising. One of the primary differences between the fighting effectiveness of a modern combat sport like judo and traditional martial arts like *jujutsu* is in the value of the training methods. Because of their potential danger or lethality, many martial arts techniques must be practiced using artificial, even counter-productive, methods. Slow, careful, non-contact training is not the most effective approach to prepare for actual fighting situations that usually require the opposite reactions.

The more potentially damaging a technique is, the more carefully and unrealistically it needs to be practiced. For example, full-contact training in throat strikes or eye gouges is seldom seen in martial arts classes, but such moves are often recommended for self-defense, even without the opportunity for the type of realistic training that would develop the skills necessary to make such techniques effective in a high-pressure situation.

Teaching these techniques may help judo students to understand intellectually what to do, but it does not provide effective results for quick, reflexive and accurate application against an unwilling opponent in real-life combat. They are simply too dangerous to practice repeatedly against a classmate.

By focusing on less dangerous defenses, sport training methods ironically result in better results for the development of combat skills. Sport more typically produces efficient, fast and spontaneous reactions with full power. Sport training achieves results against a resistant opponent, who is also utilizing full power while engaging in strategic and tactical resistance, using all of his physical ability and training. Techniques that do not work are soon abandoned, and successful skills are honed against different attackers under a variety of conditions.

Maintaining control in various combat situations – both attack and defense – is difficult when faced with the unpredictable nature of an opponent's efforts. Facing these situations in contest or practice sparring (*randori*) prepares judo students for similar situations. Each opponent in competition is operating at the limit of physical and psychological skill. By pushing that limit, contestants are continually realizing

The give and take required in judo helps participants to develop good sportsmanship.

WHAT IS JUDO?

Judo is a fusion of ancient combat art, modern sports training, and a philosophy of continuous improvement. It is a complex combat system that preserves martial traditions and techniques of Japan, but is also a popular sport that clearly prepares the athlete for any physical confrontation off the mat. It is a safe and fun recreational activity that emphasizes building character. It is an art that allows free expression and displays the beauty of coordinated movement. It is a method of training the body and mind using principles that can also apply to how you lead your life. Both sport and martial art, judo has unique depth and strength not readily found in other sports or martial arts.

and expanding their potential, preparing them mentally and physically for any serious conflict.

Training in martial arts is most effective when you can achieve objective results. It can be misleading to substitute your own subjective perception of effectiveness with a cooperating partner for an objective defeat of a resisting opponent. Practitioners of the older styles of *jujutsu* had a limited ability to train effectively for self-defense and combat during times of peace because they could not prepare for combat without severe risk to co-operative training partners. As a result, classical martial arts adopted highly stylized, ritualistic – even dysfunctional – training methods. Instead, modern combat sports like judo now provide the superior training in effective fighting techniques under real conditions.

The focus in judo training is developing effective techniques, but an important element is also the development of a fighting spirit. The ability to face a larger, more powerful, or more advanced opponent without fear requires practice in standing up to an adversary. It takes many failures and defeats before expertise can be expected. Competitiveness helps overcome these challenges and forges a courageous spirit as well as the body. The resulting confidence earned from real practice meeting diversity in the form of attack and defense carries over to other aspects of life where conflict and competition must sometimes be met squarely.

Using sport competition as preparation for real fighting can be quite different from playing it as a game. Judo matches, along with *randori* in class, are simply different methods for training the mind and body to deal with fighting situations. This helps prepare students for anything they have to fight for – whether it is fighting for their country in the Olympics, their life on the street, or any worthy goal outside of judo.

Of course, sports training can go wrong. As Jigoro Kano warned, winning and losing can become too important and start to pervert the training process. This can be manifested in many ways, such as a narrow focus on only a few techniques or building a strategy around competition rules.

The ultimate goal in judo is not winning medals, although they are certainly motivating and prized as an objective recognition of your progress and skill. The rewards and disappointments of competition help push participants to higher levels of training. Testing yourself in competition is a valuable part of the learning process. Competing in tournaments takes a commitment that ensures you will always leave the competition area with important lessons to inform your training, improve your ability and, win or lose, help to develop fighting spirit, good sportsmanship and character.

Progressing in judo

Judo is difficult to learn. Fortunately, it can also be fun. Judo is designed to be an activity anyone can participate in: from schoolchildren to seniors, from the most fit athletes to those who need to get in shape, able-bodied or physically challenged, male or female, big or small.

All students go through well-defined steps to learn the basics, and there are clear methods for working towards mastery. Whatever your limitations, success in judo can be achieved. Some of that success will only come through hard work, but much of it will come while enjoying the games, drills, free practice and tournaments common to judo around the world. Judo students feel the exhilaration of succeeding through personal effort, the joy of achieving goals, and camaraderie with others facing the same battles.

Overcoming challenges is part of what makes judo so rewarding. Sprains, scrapes, sore muscles

Through concentrated effort, learn effortless action.

and bruised egos are common in classes where beginners are learning methods of attack and defense. Some people experience emotions brought on by fatigue, defeat or apparent lack of progress. Yet students also learn that obstacles of all types can be overcome, physical limitations can be extended, and fears can be faced. This is invaluable training for anyone striving to be confident and successful.

Learning judo is a growth process. As a beginner, you learn safety rules and falling skills. You progress to learning basic positions for throwing or pinning. When you feel confident in performing basic techniques, your training partner adds movement or resistance to make it more realistic, and you learn ways of defending against attacks. You then begin to make your moves more powerful and adaptable, and learn ways of combining techniques. Next you try to apply what you have learned in *randori*, in which your training partner tries to unbalance and weaken you to facilitate your defeat. As you continue to learn more techniques and develop a greater depth of understanding of the techniques, you may be ready to test yourself in a tournament.

After each tournament or match you must re-examine your training, then redouble your efforts to study judo so you can perform better next time against an even more skilled opponent. Since every judo student is striving to improve, each brings other students along on the path to higher quality judo. You will continue to advance, perhaps exceeding your own expectations, because other students who are equally committed will help to push you to be the best that you can be.

Rely on your *sensei*, an experienced instructor, to help and guide you as you advance. The *sensei* usually has a better perspective on your training than you do, and can observe and judge your progress.

Judo is an endless path of self-discovery. It represents a journey with a definite beginning and middle, but no real end. The beginning is when you take your first few lessons, but the middle portion of the journey never ceases. A student

Adversity does not cause a judo student to wither, it helps the student flourish.

who stays on the path will always be learning and advancing. Many judo masters continue to learn new things, and approach practice with the same awe and wonder they had as new students.

In judo you first learn to control your body, your emotions and your mind; only then can you control your opponent. It is exciting the first time you throw a resisting opponent spontaneously and without effort, or hold and control someone on the ground so that he or she cannot escape from you or attempt to hurt you. As you improve you will see that techniques that seem difficult can actually be done effortlessly, even against opponents bigger than you. The more you understand about judo and the more you improve your skill level, the more fun judo is. Imagine how wonderful it feels when judo techniques come easily and they work on even the toughest opponents.

What does a black belt really mean?

One of the questions most often asked by beginners is, "How long does it take to get a black belt in judo?" Most people want to hear that it takes just a year or two of attendance in class, but the truth is that misconceptions about what a black belt is tend to give students unrealistic expectations.

In some martial arts today we see black belts worn by young children who can become a "champion" in tournaments with black belt divisions for five and six year old competitors. Martial arts schools sell contracts promising a black belt within a short time. Mail-order black belts are for sale online and people falsify certificates to claim rank they didn't earn. Celebrities are awarded honorary black belts. We see demonstrations of black belt skill involving walking on nails, swallowing swords, breaking bricks of ice, and other amazing feats. This threatens the legitimacy of martial arts ranks and raises general questions about the meaning of the black belt.

The significance of the black belt rank has been diluted over time in many martial arts

systems, particularly due to commercialism, but the worldwide standard in judo has remained quite high. As the first martial art to award belt ranks, judo students are generally required to meet minimum time-in-grade training requirements, pass promotion exams, demonstrate tournament success, maintain a moral code, and attain a minimum age.

Essentially, a judo black belt is a symbol of a student's graduation to more advanced training – one that will be even longer than the previous steps.

The first level of black belt is called *shodan*, which means first level or beginning step. Promotion to black belt recognizes hard work and a level of accomplishment of which you can be proud. But *shodan* is really just the beginning, or base, for learning the most important lessons of judo. It shows you are proficient at most of the techniques, but does not necessarily make you a qualified instructor or mean you have mastered judo.

To get a black belt you simply find a good teacher and begin training. A school in a convenient location helps you attend regularly, and a wide range of serious training partners also helps. Most importantly, you must devote yourself to practice and work hard. It is not easy, but it is a step-by-step training process, and you may attain the belt some day when you are no longer even looking for it. It could take a few years, or you may never achieve it. Black belt candidates often realize that the belt is not as important as the lessons learned along the way.

Ranks are earned by the student, but awarded by the instructor. The instructor can recognize all the factors that make up a black belt and should be trusted to promote you when you have demonstrated the required skills. As you master the physical skills and techniques, you will also likely exhibit improvements in conduct, character, maturity and internalization of the principles of judo.

Applying judo principles to life outside judo school is something that brings judo black belts together. This is one of the reasons Jigoro Kano renamed his style of *jujutsu,* calling it judo. *Do* means the way, path or road that students of judo follow. In other words, it is more than just the activity that takes place on the mat. As a judo black belt, you will begin to understand how the principles you have learned in class can improve your character and impact the rest of your life. For example, when you learn through experience to be committed to the successful application of a judo throw and to follow through to completion, you become conscious of how these same fundamentals of commitment and follow through can help you to achieve other goals off the mats.

Continuously striving for perfection as a whole person is a sign of the black belt. This is not to say that black belts do not have faults – they are just the ones working hardest on improving themselves. All judo black belts would affirm how learning judo has helped them change their lives for the better. The belt simply represents their personal struggle to achieve excellence.

Students who are overly concerned with getting promotions often discourage easily when they realize it is harder than they expected. Those who strive for excellence without concern for rank often do well; they are not affected by temporary setbacks or discouraged by unrealistic expectations. The road to black belt begins with enthusiasm – if you have the persistence and dedication to pursue ever-greater accomplishments your enthusiasm will only gwrow.

Goals of judo training

People have different goals for their participation in judo. These range from being the best in the world and winning a gold medal at the Olympics, to learning basic self-defense, just having fun, or developing self-confidence so you will not be afraid. As you advance in judo your goals may change. One of the wonderful things about judo is that there are multiple levels of principles and goals: a beginner can focus on mastering a single hip throw, while a more advanced student doing the same hip throw gains insight into the larger meaning of judo.

Judo in a narrow sense is the study of the most efficient and effective methods of attack and defense. One goal of judo as physical education is to develop a healthy mind and body that work harmoniously together. Another is to work with others in synergy so everyone benefits. Ultimately, by striving for perfection you can contribute something of value and improve the world we live in. Essentially, the goals of judo involve improving yourself physically, mentally and morally. They also involve ethical and social principles that Jigoro Kano believed were implicit by-products of judo training.

Judo teaches you to be present on the battlefield of life, ready to meet any challenge.

CHAPTER 2:
STARTING JUDO

Like all forms of physical education, judo is designed so that dedicated students can become proficient over time. The training methods and physical principles that make judo work apply to women and men equally, and to all ages from young children to senior citizens. Judo is a strong component of both the Olympic Games and the Paralympic Games (for outstanding blind athletes). No one is too tall or too short, too heavy or too light, too strong or too weak. People of all backgrounds from all parts of the world practice judo together with minimal equipment and expense. The most basic requirement is the will to learn.

In the beginning

The way to learn judo is through training – that is, to become proficient with specialized instruction and practice. You cannot achieve this on your own. To become skilled in judo you must find an expert instructor to teach you, and other students with whom to practice. The choice of a school, or *dojo*, may vary depending on your age, interests and condition, but since there are many experienced judo teachers, or *sensei*, it should not be hard to locate one near you. Judo is generally one of the most affordable martial arts you can participate in. The online resources listed in the appendix can help you with that.

If you have multiple choices, choose the *dojo* that inspires you to attend every class. When you don't attend class your skills regress, while everyone else improves, making it harder for you to keep up. It is no secret that attending class is the most important prerequisite to progress. So find a *dojo* that is conveniently located and which you enjoy going to.

Preparing for class

Even before trying some of the skills you want to learn as a new student, you should understand the class rules and etiquette so that you feel comfortable participating. The *dojo* is a welcoming place, but you want to fit in by learning some of the customs.

In addition to a *dojo* with proper mats, you only need a *judogi* to begin. Your *dojo* will usually be able to recommend one and help you get it. The *judogi* is made of strong cotton fabric which is loose and comfortable to exercise in. It is an essential part of judo because it is used to manipulate your partner. The traditional *judogi* is white, but competitors may also need a blue *judogi* for some tournaments.

In preparation for every practice the first thing you do is put on your *judogi* which is made of three parts: a heavy jacket (*uwagi*), pants (*zubon*), and belt (*obi*).

The pants use a simple drawstring to tighten the waist. The front of the *zubon* has one or two

Ten things you should know about your *sensei*

1. Your *sensei* loves judo. This is the reason he or she wants to practice and teach.

2. Your *sensei* wants to share judo with everyone. It is a valuable gift that should be shared.

3. Your *sensei* knows that Judo is not easy to learn. It takes hard work and a considerable amount of time. Your *sensei* has been through this training and understands the commitment needed. Your *sensei* wants you to be even better than him or her.

4. Your *sensei* wants the training to be safe. Because there are inherent risks in judo practice, all students must put safety above all other short-term goals.

5. You are important to the *sensei*. There would be no judo without students of all levels, and every student is important. This is part of the judo principle of mutual welfare and benefit.

6. Your *sensei* can be trusted to guide your instruction. Your *sensei* carefully prepares lessons and will make adjustments for individual and class performance levels. However, in the beginning everything may not be clear to you, so patience is required.

7. Since your *sensei* wants to improve, he or she benefits from having the opportunity to practice judo with you. One of the goals of judo is to continuously strive to improve yourself so that you can contribute to the world. If you are having difficulty in class, or thinking of quitting, discuss it with your sensei so that he or she can learn from your point of view.

8. Your *sensei* wants you to study outside of class. The more you read, practice, and learn on your own, the more valuable your class time will be. Keep yourself physically fit with additional conditioning outside of class.

9. Your *sensei* needs your help. Your class will benefit from helping other students along, caring for the mats, assisting with tournaments, etc.

10. For your *sensei*, judo is a way of life.

Jacket *(uwagi)* — Lapel *(eri)*
Sleeve *(sode)*
Skirt *(suso)* — Belt *(obi)*
Pants *(zubon)*

loops so you can pass the strings through it. These are tied in the front (a bow is sufficient), and the ends of the string should be tucked inside the pants. Pants should reach your ankle and not drag on the ground.

The jacket is a strong, heavy, cotton weave that closes in front with your left side over the right side. Sleeves should come to the wrist, and the back should cover your buttocks. It is held closed by tying the belt around your waist with a square knot.

Since we practice judo barefoot, bring a pair of sandals to wear whenever you are not on the mat. This helps keep the mat clean.

The *dojo* is a serious place for martial arts training, and deserves your adherence to the *dojo* rules which are there mostly to protect students. Every *dojo* has rules for behavior, so find out about the rules for your specific class. Here is an example of a Code of Conduct for a judo class:

- The rules and etiquette of judo must be scrupulously respected. This includes showing up on time prepared to begin.

- All participants will act in a sportsmanlike manner consistent with the spirit of fair play.

- Participants will conduct themselves in an ethical manner that will not in any way bring disrespect, discredit, or dishonor to themselves or our dojo.

- All participants will exercise self-control and remain disciplined in all circumstances. Show respect for people and facilities. Students are expected to follow instructions from the instructor to the best or their abilities.
- All practice should be in accordance with the judo principle of mutual welfare and benefit. Therefore, safety is a primary consideration in practice.
- Due to risk of injury, members are not to use judo techniques outside of class. Keep fingernails and toenails trimmed. Do not bring hard or metallic objects on the mat. Immediately report any injuries.
- Cleanliness is important in judo, as in all contact sports. Arrive with a clean *judogi*. Wear sandals at all times off the mat, and never go on the mat with shoes. Food, drinks and chewing gum are not permitted on the mat.
- Participants are expected to contribute by assisting with all activities such as caring for the mats, paying dues timely, and keeping the facility clean.
- All forms of harassment, bullying, hazing, or abuse are prohibited be it physical, verbal, emotional, or otherwise.

Your first class

Enter the *dojo* with a positive attitude, ready to try your best. From the first class you will begin to learn some of the safety rules and etiquette of judo. Safety must always be a consideration if judo is to bring you long-term health benefits, not injuries. Because judo is a very effective combat sport, some of the techniques can hurt a classmate if they are not applied carefully and properly. Dangerous techniques should not be practiced outside class or on someone who is unprepared. In class, safety requires everyone to focus on what he or she is doing, and to treat training partners with care. Your approach to practice should always be conscientious and determined.

RULES OF THE DOJO BY KYUZO MIFUNE, 1883-1965

Have no falsehood in mind.
Reluctance or deceit are not conducive to the inner harmony required by judo practice.

Do not lose self-confidence.
Learn to act wholeheartedly, without hesitation. Show reverence toward the practice of judo, by keeping your mind in it.

Keep your balance.
The center of gravity follows the movement of the body. The center of gravity is the most important element in maintaining stablility. If it is lost, the body is naturally unbalanced. Thus, fix your mind so that your body is always in balance.

Utilize your strength efficiently.
Minimize the use of strength with the quickest movement of body. Acknowledge that what is called stillness and motion is nothing but an endlessly repeated process.

Don't discontinue training.
Mastery of judo cannot be accomplished in a short time. Since skills depend on mental and physical application, constant training is essential.

Keep yourself humble.
If you become self-centered, you will build a wall around yourself and lose your freedom. If you can humble yourself in preparation for an event you will surely be better able to judge and understand it. In a match, you will be able to detect the weak point of your opponent and easily put him/her under control.

Since judo is a Japanese martial art, practice will expose you to a few Japanese customs, bowing is the most important. Your first bow (*rei*) may be upon entering the *dojo* for your class. Bow again when you step on the mat, when the class begins, before and after practice with each partner, when the class ends, and finally when you leave the mat area and the *dojo*.

Classes customarily begin and end with a bow intended to show respect and appreciation for your *dojo, sensei* and training partners. As class begins, focus your attention like you need to do in a self-defense situation. Observe carefully and concentrate on what you are doing. Your state of awareness will be a huge factor in your success, and training begins with focusing your attention while bowing.

Each person you practice with gives their body to you, and trusts that you will take care not to injure them. Bowing is an agreement between participants to try their best to improve, with equal consideration for the progress and safety of both partners.

Proper judo etiquette (*reiho*) is vital in a combat sport to prevent it from devolving into a fight where winning is the only important goal. The bow reminds us that we are all keeping the principle of mutual welfare and benefit in mind. When you and your partner begin practice together the bow expresses the greeting, "Let's improve ourselves together through this training." The bow at the end of practice is an expression of gratitude, "Thank you for being my partner."

There are two primary ways to bow, sitting (*zarei*) and standing (*ritsurei*). *Rei* is the Japanese word for bow used as a command to tell the class when to bow. You will see others in class bowing, so it is easy to learn the proper distance, posture, and etiquette. Being observant in class is a good habit that will help you quickly pick up on skills, so start right away and copy the good behavior of the most experienced members of your class.

The bow is typically followed by a warm-up period with strength, flexibility, coordination, and other exercises to improve your fitness level while learning skills that will be helpful. Judo practice alone will improve your fitness level (after all it is designed as a complete system of physical education) but generally speaking the better condition you are in, the better you will become at judo. Both aerobic and non-aerobic exercise will be valuable to supplement your judo training. Most serious athletes supplement their sport specific training with specialized stretching, weight training, cardio or other vigorous exercise; judo athletes are no exception. Your fitness level can either limit your training or speed it up, and it is an element that can be important for safety in class. Injuries will be less frequent, and recovery will often be quicker, if you keep your fitness level high.

The Professor took the old practices and studied them, worked out their mechanical principles and then devised a graded scientific set of tricks, based on the elementary laws of mechanics, a study of the equilibrium of the human body, the ways in which it is disturbed, how to recover your own and take advantage of the shifting of the center of gravity of the other person. The first thing that is taught is how to fall down without being hurt, that alone is worth the price of admission and ought to be taught in all our gyms.
　　　　　　　　　　　　　　　　—John Dewey

It is impossible to enjoy judo practice if you are afraid of falling, or if you get hurt while falling. As most people are naturally afraid of falling, it takes considerable practice and specific skills to overcome this obstacle. The good news is that you get immediate feedback in the form of pain when you do not perform the skill correctly, so listening to your body allows you to improve and refine your technique, along with the help of your instructor and lots of repetition.

In most throws partners will hold onto each other until a landing is safely accomplished so the fall is controlled and supported, but you begin learning to fall by yourself in a step by step

Learning how to fall

Ukemi is the art of breaking your fall to land safely when thrown to the mat. It is an important skill to master in order to make your participation in judo safe and fun. *Ukemi* is also valuable to protect yourself off the mat by preparing you to minimize injury from an unexpected or accidental fall. Becoming an expert at falling provides a life-long benefit. According to the U.S. Centers for Disease Control and Prevention one out of four Americans over age 65 experience a fall each year resulting in 3 million emergency department visits for serious injuries such as broken bones or head injuries. Judo training in strength, flexibility, and balance can help prevent falls, while *ukemi* practice helps reduce the injuries involved.

Typical side fall position after throw

Back fall

Side fall

Forward roll

process under the supervision of your *sensei*. Most judo classes include time for all participants to regularly practice their *ukemi*. You will see black belts continue to practice falls because you must prepare for the countless situations when you might need them.

Judo throwing techniques should only be practiced with a person who is skillful in *ukemi*. While the person throwing *(tori)* must exercise caution and control, the person falling *(uke)* must also accept a successful throw and fall with skill. This shared responsibility is representative of the mutual welfare we exercise to keep judo practice safe.

Being able to fall comfortably and with confidence frees the mind and relaxes the body so you can attempt more difficult moves. You simply cannot attack or defend freely unless you master *ukemi*. Performing a throw involves both applying a technique and receiving a technique. *Ukemi* is the art of receiving an attack by controlling how you land when a fall is inevitable, sometimes going with the flow, sometimes twisting out of a score, but always landing safely.

There are many types of *ukemi*, but essentially you need to develop the ability to fall in every direction and land safely. You may fall forward, backwards, and on your right or left side for a successful throw, and sometimes face down for an unsuccessful throw. In each direction you learn both rolling and falling flat on the mat.

One distinctive element of *ukemi* is the slap. If you land on your right side, slap the mat with your entire right arm to decelerate, taking up the force of the fall. This technique also prevents you from reaching out and getting injuring by landing on your arm. When you fall on your back, slap with both arms.

The judo rank system

Jigoro Kano created the basic ranking system that is still used in almost all martial arts today. This rank system replaced the traditional scrolls or diplomas used in older martial arts. He is also responsible for creating the basic white training uniform used in judo which was later adapted for other martial arts like *karate* and *aikido*. Utilizing the belt to recognize ranks with different colors was an innovation that gave participants an outward sign of the experience level of instructors

The black belt is a symbol of individual growth and accomplishment.

The red-and-white belt is worn by 6th, 7th and 8th degree black belts.

and fellow students. The black belt (*dan* rank) was the first rank created. It signified completion of the first step of training. There are ten levels of black belt for further advancement. The number of ranks and colored belts have expanded over time.

Before concerning yourself with the black belt, there are several student ranks (*kyu* grades) to earn. Each rank is represented with a different color belt, which may be accompanied by a certificate or other proof of rank. Traditionally there are six *kyu* grades, with first *kyu* the highest rank, but rank systems used in different countries, organizations, locales, and even individual instructors vary. Typically, belts awarded to children are more numerous and come quicker for the motivation and recognition they provide.

Promotions are earned by taking an examination, and/or excellent performance in class and contests. There is a range of skill exhibited by students of the same rank, just like students who are all in the same grade at school. But every student who is promoted to a new rank is better than they were in the previous rank, and all students should have a basic competency that prepares them for more advanced education.

CHAPTER 3:
JUDO TRAINING METHODS

The primary types of traditional judo training are *kata*, *randori*, and *shiai* (which may be considered a special form of *randori*). *Uchikomi*, *nagekomi* and drills are used to hone techniques through repetition until they can be applied spontaneously. In addition, there are countless games and exercises designed to develop specific skills.

Kata

Kata means form, and is a method of practicing with a cooperating partner in a prearranged fashion, following a basic pattern created by experts to teach specific skills and combative principles. It is often seen as a formal demonstration, in special *kata* tournaments, or as an advanced rank promotion requirement, but is also an important exercise in judo class. It is in the practice of *kata* that you develop a wide range of judo skills seldom used or not allowed in *randori* or *shiai*, including different throws, joint locks, combat ranges, striking and pressure points. Students learn to apply techniques to both sides in response to a diverse set of attacks, which may even include an assortment of weapons such as a handgun or a Japanese dagger called a *tanto*.

The *randori no kata* are the most commonly practiced *kata* because they involve the techniques that are most often performed in free practice and they complement the study of many popular throwing and grappling techniques. The techniques included in the *randori no kata* are listed in the appendix. The other *kata* are usually required for promotion to higher black belt ranks.

The Kodokan *kata* help preserve a worldwide standard for judo techniques and theory. Practicing them provides students with a connection to Jigoro Kano and others who devised them. They help with in-depth study of techniques with a partner learning the same techniques, so that you develop cooperative skills to balance the competitive ones learned in other forms of training. Cooperation in *kata* practice does not mean your training partner is acting a part; it just means that *uke* (person receiving the technique) has agreed to perform certain attacks in a specified manner. Each attack *uke* makes is intended to be successful and it is up to *tori* (person performing the technique) to apply the proper defense.

Sharpen your sword in *randori* so that it will be capable of one swift cut when needed.

The level of resistance and effort in *randori* should always be adjusted to the size and ability of your partner, so that you work harder against larger or more skilled partners and stay lighter against smaller or less skilled partners.

Practice partners in *randori* are often competing to gain the advantage and do not know what the other will do, so they must be prepared to make quick judgments and act decisively. Jigoro Kano wrote about the

A comprehensive study of *kata* also consists of important combat concepts such as the concentration of spirit (*kiai*), judgment of engagement distance (*maai*), performance of appropriate action in conformance with combat theory (*riai*), and the establishment of a special kind of alertness to dominate the opponent (*zanshin*). If all the techniques comprise the alphabet of judo, then *kata* represents the complete words, as well as the basic grammar and sentence structure.

Randori

Students practicing *randori*, or free practice, are learning to use the letters, words and sentences of judo to communicate in a meaningful way. The meaning of the Japanese word *randori* suggests there is generally no controlling form or pre-established method of practice. It is often practiced freely, with each person attacking and defending at will with full power. At other times it is practiced lightly with less resistance, or with restrictions to train in a particular area of study (for example, grappling on the mat from a selected starting position such as hands and knees).

Seoi nage in Ju no Kata

"hundreds of valuable lessons" of *randori* in *Kodokan Judo*:

> *In randori one can never be sure what technique the opponent will employ next, so he must be constantly on guard. Being alert becomes second nature. One acquires poise, the self-confidence that comes from knowing that he can cope with any eventuality. The powers of attention and observation, imagination, of reasoning and judgment are naturally heightened, and these are all useful attributes in daily life as well as in the dojo.*

It is generally accepted by judo experts, including Jigoro Kano, that *randori* must be given priority in your training. It adds an element of realism to judo and should be the mainstay of practice time once you have learned the basics. *Randori* involves a complex mental and physical relationship between the participants that *kata* cannot achieve. There is a huge difference between learning how to do a technique with a cooperating partner and being able to apply it with minimum effort against a well-trained, resisting opponent. Only in *randori* do you learn how to take advantage of opportunities created by your opponent's movements, reactions, posture, strength and composure. *Randori* is more about constantly improving yourself than doing everything right, so do not be afraid to try a variety of techniques.

Randori is driven by the energy of discovery born of risk and error. As you attempt to attack you will often fail, but as Jigoro Kano said, "When you fall down seven times, get up eight." *Randori* is the time to create opportunities and see possibilities, overcoming your limitations. The value of judo is gained, like food, only upon digestion and assimilation. It can only be appreciated through experience – and *randori* provides the practical, free environment to experience all that judo has to offer. Eventually, *randori* will lead to a new understanding of proper technique, and a state of awareness that will allow quick, reflexive and decisive action. Rather than thinking about your next move, it is better to be so present in the realities of the moment so you simply act in harmony with the flow of the match.

Top tips for *randori*

Success in *randori* is one sign that a student is ready for the black belt rank. Here is some of the most common advice judo teachers give to help students with their *randori*.

- There is no score or winner in *randori*, so banish thoughts of victory or defeat.
- Focus on attacking freely without regard for being thrown.
- Keep a relaxed and natural posture to retain free movement of your body and mind.
- Keep your arms loose.
- Keep your head up and centered over your hips.
- Do not waste energy.
- Follow through with each technique; do not get in the habit of going half way.
- Follow up each technique with another.
- Never refuse a practice partner.
- Seek out training partners who are better than you.
- Try new moves to overcome problem situations.
- Use *kiai* (concentration of your spirit in a shout) for extra power.
- Rely on skill and timing, not strength.
- Control your breathing.
- Keep your elbows close to your body where they are most powerful and least vulnerable.
- Always face your opponent.
- Do not cross your feet when moving around.
- Get the strongest grip you can, and never fail to get a grip.
- Learn to feel your partner's intentions and anticipate attacks.
- Maintain *mizu no kokoro* (mind like water); stay calm and undisturbed.
- Focus on *kuzushi* (breaking balance) to create opportunities for attacks.
- Employ the principle of maximum efficiency even when you could easily overpower the opponent with size or strength.
- Help your partner to learn while you perfect your technique.
- Act now; analyze later.
- Do not make excuses; do not give up. Tomorrow you will be better.

Shiai

Shiai, or contest, is a vital component of a well-developed course in judo. It is the form of judo practice you will spend the least amount of time actually doing, but you may spend the most amount of time preparing for. In tournaments you use all your previous training to overcome an opponent who is doing his or her best to defeat you. Even in small local tournaments the pressure to succeed creates a very different environment from friendly practice in class.

Valuable lessons can be learned in *shiai*, including some that cannot be gained in other forms of practice. Judo is a unique face-to-face form of individual competition involving

Sharpen your sword in *randori* so that it will be capable of one swift cut when needed.

Learn from the mistakes of others, you may not live long enough to make them all yourself.

full contact attack and defense. Fighting is an acquired skill, but learning to stand up to others, and to fight fairly with resolve for what you believe in, will serve you well not only in judo but throughout life.

As you progress in judo, continue to challenge yourself by seeking better competition.

One purpose of competition in judo is to take the place of the older *shinken shobu* (life-and-death fights) in developing your technique, knowledge and character. You never see yourself so clearly as when you face your own death. Judo competition can provide a safe, controlled glimpse at this kind of defeat – and the level of effort required to win.

Fighting spirit can really only be developed through fighting. Certainly, judo competition is not the same as fighting on the battlefield, but it is closer to a hand-to-hand combat situation than any other safe form of training for the ordinary person. It prepares you to fight to protect yourself or others, and focuses the development of your judo skills.

Judo students should be aware that winning at all costs is not the proper attitude for entering judo *shiai*. When used as a training method, judo competition is not about winning or losing; it is about giving your best effort and improving yourself, challenging yourself to stretch beyond your own self-imposed limits. No one ever developed any real confidence without first overcoming significant personal challenges.

Participating in *shiai* is like placing a red-hot blade under the hammer of a swordsmith to sharpen it. In this sense it is a form of *seishin tanren*, or spiritual forging. It is about testing yourself and helping your opponent to do the same. By testing your skills under pressure you learn to improve your level of ability, focus your preparation and training, and strengthen your mental toughness. This further increases the self-confidence and fighting spirit being developed during *kata* and *randori* practice.

The rules of judo competition have changed considerably since the first Kodokan Red and

As you progress in judo, continue to challenge yourself by seeking better competition.

White Tournament was held in 1884. At first, Kodokan judo was seen as a form of *jujutsu* and matches were held in the older *jujutsu* style. An early participant in these matches, Sakujiro Yokoyama, is quoted as saying:

> *In those days contests were extremely rough and frequently cost the participants their lives. Thus, whenever I sallied forth to take part in any of those affairs, I invariably bade farewell to my parents, since I had no assurance that I should ever return alive.*

The rules of judo were created by Jigoro Kano, but have been revised many times. Locks of the fingers, toes, wrists and ankles were banned in contests in 1899. In 1916, *ashi garami* (knee entanglement, twisting knee lock) and *dojime* (trunk/kidney squeeze with the legs) were also banned in competition. Joint lock attacks in judo contests were limited to the elbow in 1925. Over the years other rules have also been created to ensure the safety of contestants – such as the banning of *kani basami* (flying scissors) after this throw injured Japanese champion Yasuhiro Yamashita's ankle.

Judo matches originally had no weight categories and no time limit. It was not until 1964, when judo competition was recognized as an event in the Olympic Games, that judo competition was divided into three weight classes. The World Championship finals still lasted up to 15 minutes until the 1970s. As judo became more popular, the number of weight classes increased to seven for both men and women, and match times were reduced to the current five minute limit. Notably the All Japan Championships are still conducted in the traditional manner with no weight classes.

The International Judo Federation (IJF) is recognized by the International Olympic Committee as the governing body for Olympic judo. Since 1952 it has established the rules of judo competition and administered the sport.

Each country has a national judo organization that is a member of the IJF. As a result, the rules of judo *shiai* are very consistent around the world, except for special safety rules for children or novices that may vary from country to country.

Other forms of training

Beginners usually start learning judo techniques with partners in a form of practice that is called *uchikomi*, or repetition training, performed in a cooperative fashion to achieve the basic movement patterns. This is the first step to gaining the physical coordination and understanding of a throw or other judo technique. It consists of entering into the position for applying a technique, usually a throw, but stopping short of executing it. Repeating the movement over and over again gets the throw ingrained into the muscles and mind so that the essential preparatory movements of the throw can be done quickly and spontaneously, without thinking.

Feedback is important so that correct technique is reinforced in uchikomi practice.

Judo training helps you to be self-disciplined, attentive and considerate of others; the more you practice these character traits outside class the better.

Uchikomi allows you to learn new throws when you do not yet have sufficient control to complete them safely. Even after you are skilled in a throw, *uchikomi* is a popular form of practice because you get many repetitions focusing on some important elements of a technique – such as breaking balance or the application of power – without much falling for your training partner.

While *uchikomi* is repetition of the movements entering into a technique, *nagekomi* is the repeated practice of the entire throwing technique. In *nagekomi*, you repeatedly throw your opponent to the mat. This essential form of practice adds the vital steps for application and follow through for each technique. A thick landing mat, or crash pad, may sometimes be used to make repeated hard falling more comfortable and to protect both partners.

Yakusoku geiko is an agreed-upon or controlled form of practice where participants decide in advance what the conditions will be. One traditional method of applying this to *randori* is to agree to practice throws without resistance from the partner while alternating attackers, so that each person gets a turn to practice completing a variety of throws. Practice partners may also agree to allow a certain degree of resistance, or allow throw avoidance but not counter throws, or any other restriction to focus the training on the desired area of practice.

Variations of these traditional practices have been devised to build competency by training repetitively in a specific aspect of judo performance. For example, one person in *randori* can be designated the attacker while the other practices a particular defense, or a student can work for a designated period of time against a common defense (like stiff-arming) to master the numerous skills for defeating it. *Uchikomi* can be done on a moving partner to develop essential timing through more realistic situations than

Tips for solo practice

Judo students often wonder how they can practice without a partner. A general strength and conditioning programme is beneficial, and all serious judo students should try to improve their fitness levels with additional training outside class. Although most judo techniques require a practice partner, there are a few ways to improve some skills by yourself.

• Practice the footwork needed to enter for throws. Try placing bricks in front of you to represent your opponent's feet, then repeatedly step or jump into position for various hip, leg or shoulder throws. Try the same steps with your hands against a wall, or in a swimming pool with your legs under water.

• Tie a bicycle tire inner tube (or your judo belt) around a post or tree. Grab one end with each hand, and practice entering for your favourite throw as in uchikomi. A thousand repetitions will improve the strength, speed and accuracy of your entry. This can be done with cable weights to improve strength, or with the inner tube tied to something that moves (like an open door handle) to improve balance.

• To practice judo techniques, some students buy grappling dummies – commercially produced mannequins with lifelike weight, movable joints and a tough exterior. They are especially useful for repetitive drills on the ground.

Remember, perfect technique comes only from perfect practice. When a teacher is not around, do not develop bad habits. Constantly examine your practice to ensure you are performing each move correctly.

Left: Grab the belt as if it is your opponent's jacket and practice entering for throws with good posture and driving power.

Right: Using bricks (or sandals) in various positions as though they were your opponent's feet, jump into different throws to increase speed, accuracy and balance.

static *uchikomi* provides. *Nagekomi* may be done with multiple partners to practice a quick grip and throw sequence. Attacks in *kata* may be speeded up to improve responses under stress.

A good judo coach has ways of training athletes for each distinct skill or competitive tactic that needs to be strengthened. For maximum transference to real competition, these drills should duplicate the specific biomechanics, neuromuscular patterns, pressures and other conditions commonly faced in competition (or self-defense situations).

Many other drills, both individual and with a partner, have been devised to train participants in particular skills of judo, such as gripping, turning over an opponent on the ground, throwing while moving, and so on. Modern sports methodology is often used to train high performance judo athletes, and scientific advances in sports training methods have added new concepts to some of the traditional judo training methods, particularly for Olympic and elite competitors.

CHAPTER 4:
WHY JUDO WORKS

Judo instruction stresses application over theory. A real understanding of the principles that make judo work is revealed slowly through long and sometimes arduous practice. Full comprehension does not come from intellectual investigation as much as from physical application, which can only be achieved through proper training. However, you can proceed with the knowledge that judo has been studied extensively and there is a sound basis for the successful application of the various attacks.

"We can say that Judo is an art because it is a method of arriving at self-realization and true self-expression. We can further say that Judo is a science because it implies mastery of various laws of nature: gravity, friction, momentum, velocity, weight transmission, and unison of forces."

— *The Art and Science of Judo* by Jiichi Watanabe and Lindy Avakian

Scientific basis

Judo is a modern combat sport based on scientific principles. A principle is simply a rule explaining the functioning of a natural phenomenon. In judo combat, it is advisable to use the most natural and intuitive solution possible so that your response is fluid and efficient.

Jigoro Kano explained the effectiveness of seemingly impossible feats with rational explanations based on sound science. Judo teachers today still stress proper technique over excessive force to achieve an objective. Good technique means the correct application of strength and other resources in accordance with natural laws and principles that maximize the results of your efforts. It is this emphasis on technique that allows a smaller person with proper training to defeat a larger or stronger person. To improve your chances of success in any form of combat one needs some advantage other than brute force alone. At the heart of judo strategy is the premise that sheer size and raw strength are no match for good balance, skill and flexibility.

The Kodokan has actively encouraged scientific studies that give greater insight into how judo works, and how it can be improved, since even before Jigoro Kano established the Association for the Medical Studies on Judo in 1932. The name of the group changed to the Association for the Scientific Studies on Judo in 1948. The areas of study include medical science, physical education, history, strength, techniques, coaching methods, and psychology.

Physical concepts utilized in judo include gravity, leverage, inertia, force, friction, velocity, acceleration, power, stability and momentum. If you understand how your anatomical center of gravity, muscular rigidity and other factors affect balance, it may be easier to learn to apply throws and other skills. Similarly, a study of basic anatomy, biomechanics and kinesiology is useful for understanding how joint locks are applied, how to make strangulations work, or where to apply pressure on the body to achieve the maximum result.

Although these laws of nature may seem puzzling as they are applied to the type of complicated human interaction we see in judo, they are learned almost intuitively through

Use science to improve your judo

Here are some specific principles judo students use to maximize their effectiveness.

- Focus the power of your entire body onto one part of your opponent's body to gain an advantaget.

- When faced with unstoppable power, yield and give way in order to use your opponent's power against him or her.

- Apply your energy in the direction your opponent is moving.

- Exploit leverage to maximize your strength.

- Attack your opponent's weakness with your strength to gain victory.

- Keep your opponent moving to build momentum.

- Maintain flexibility in your body to help keep your balance.

- Pull when pushed, push when pulled.

- Move quickly to gain a position of relative advantage.

- Get under your opponent's centre of gravity to attack.

- Keep your own centre of gravity low to defend.

- Keep a wide base when on the ground.

- Keep your body loose so the effect of your opponent's force can be localized and nullified.

- Utilize your full body length as one unit to gain the greatest leverage.

- Use your full body mass, not just the strength of your arms or legs, to increase power.

- Concentrate all of your power at the moment of attack.

- Increases the force available for attacks through speed.

- Overwhelming strength can only be used against you if you try to oppose it.

experimentation and instruction. Additional study and careful scientific analysis can improve your performance and heighten your appreciation of the complexities inherent in physical combat.

Even for beginners concentrating on learning to fall, fundamental scientific rules, such as the dissipation of energy, can explain why certain falling methods are used. Judo teachers need a solid understanding of these principles to communicate the reasons for each movement, to validate training exercises, or to show how judo works.

What might be considered small improvements can make the difference between winning and losing. Many sports utilize technologies such as slow motion video analysis, advanced opposition research and analysis, respiration and heart monitoring, wearable sensor technology, and even virtual reality exercises. The point of these tools is to maximize performance utilizing scientific analysis followed by specific training for greater efficiency. Published studies contribute to peak performance by helping you determine the best diet, optimal training exercises, how to prevent and recover from injury, and so on.

Judo is as much a science as it is an art. There is room for individual stylistic expression, and to appreciate the gracefulness and beauty of judo, but the core of judo is its effectiveness: a judo technique must work in the real world, even under unfavorable conditions. Acting in accordance with the physical laws of the universe is essential if you are to achieve the maximum result from your efforts.

Laws of motion

Understanding the physical principles involved in judo contributes to your performance by ensuring that your actions maximize the result you are seeking so you can accomplish great things without wasting your energy. Consider, for instance, Newton's laws of motion written in 1686, exactly 20 years after he developed the theory of gravity (which is also quite important in judo). Newton's laws of motion are critical to understanding how to keep your balance, or how to unbalance an opponent in preparation for a throw.

Newton's first law of motion states that every object will remain at rest, or in uniform motion in a straight line, unless compelled to change its state by the action of an external force. This is normally taken as the definition of inertia, which can be an obstacle to overcome when you are trying to throw someone from a static position. Applied to judo, it means that a moving opponent will tend to continue moving, so when you are executing a forward throw it is most efficient simply to stop your opponent's feet from advancing while his or her upper body continues effortlessly in the direction it was moving. This unbalances your opponent, regardless of size, without using unnecessary strength.

Newton's second law of motion explains that an object will only accelerate or decelerate if a force is acting on it. The law defines the force to be equal to the change in momentum (mass times velocity) over time. In other words, if your own body mass is moving sharply towards your opponent, the amount of force exerted on your opponent will be determined by your size, speed and how quickly you decelerate into your opponent. Your own momentum being applied as a force to your opponent is often an important factor in causing your opponent to lose balance – which is your objective. Harnessing your own mass to generate momentum is more efficient than simply using isolated muscles to create the same amount of force.

Gravity

Gravity is the force of attraction that causes objects to fall towards the center of the Earth. Power in judo comes not from your muscles, but from hitting an opponent with the Earth using the force of gravity. Aside from increasing your power, gravity helps you keep your balance, and at the same time throw someone who is imbalanced.

The center of gravity for a standing person is low in the abdomen, although it varies somewhat from person to person based on sex, posture, body type, etc. It is the balance point between the upper half of the body and the lower half.

When your center of gravity is directly over the center point between your feet, you are in balance.

The device of giving way until the proper time involves the use of perfect balance, rhythm and harmony, and perception — the kinesthetic or "sixth-sense" feel — of the opponent's off-balance movements. It is this that enables the judoist to gain eventual victory. When his opponent attacks, he must harmonize his own movements with the opponent's brute force in order to gain victory. Thus his preliminary retreat is performed with the goal of ultimate victory in mind.

—*The Art and Science of Judo,* Watanabe and Avakian

When you move your upper body, for example forward to start walking, your upper body gets ahead of your feet for an instant until you step forward and regain balance. The opportunity to enter for an attack is when the opponent is off balance, because of their own motion, your push/pull, or their posture.

In *newaza*, gravity gives an advantage to the person on top who can bear their weight down while the opponent must fight gravity to get up. It is for this reason that all *osaekomi waza* require pressure downward onto your *uke* to maximize control without wasted energy.

Stability

Stability is related to balance and describes how likely it is for a structure or person to fall. Stability is not the same thing as rigidity. Surprisingly, a tall building does not necessarily become more stable when it is strong and rigid. To absorb the forces of wind or earthquakes, a building must have some ability to flex. Understanding how to make yourself more stable requires careful study of your rigidity, posture, movement, and balance.

Several factors affect the stability of an object when outside forces are exerted on it, whether it is a building, a person standing or a person pinning.

- Height: the lower or shorter an object, the better the balance.
- Center of gravity: the closer the center of gravity to the center point of the base, the better the balance.
- Base: the wider the base in each direction, the better the balance.

- Friction: the greater the friction between the body and the ground, the more difficult it is to unbalance.
- Mass: the heavier an object, the more difficult it is to unbalance.
- Rigidity: the more flexible and responsive to external forces, the better the balance.

In order to keep yourself in balance you must consider each of these factors. When trying to pin someone, for example, keep your body low and over your base, widen your base by spreading your legs, utilize your weight to increase friction and press down on *uke*, and stay flexible so you can move and adjust as needed.

Balance

Maintaining good balance is critical to judo performance, and it is especially difficult since your opponent is constantly trying to disrupt your balance. From the start, try to understand the factors involved in balance. Experienced judo athletes are very difficult to take down because of their training. Of course, keeping your balance in judo practice is good training to prevent accidents outside of class as well.

Insight regarding balance begins with knowing how we perceive it. Before modern medical science we learned that there are 5 senses: sight, hearing, touch, taste and smell. With increased knowledge about the human body, we now know that there are many more senses. While sight and touch are critical senses for martial arts, there are even more important senses that help with balance, which partly explains why blind athletes perform so well in judo.

Your ears actually play an important role in balance. Several structures in the inner ear vestibular system send signals to the brain that help you orient yourself and maintain balance. The utricle and the saccule, monitor movements of your head from side to side and up and down, and also detect gravity which aids in the sense of up and down. Other structures monitor the rotation of your head.

While the vestibular system supplies information about head position, it does not communicate everything about the positioning of the body. Additional information comes from vision and proprioception. Vision is not essential to balance, yet we tend to rely on it to the point of making it difficult to even stand on one foot with our eyes closed. Gymnasts, martial artists, and other athletes performing similar complex physical skills must train to consider other cues. In this context, proprioception is the most important sense.

Sensory receptors in your muscles, joints, ligaments and skin help identify where your body is in space. These receptors, such as those on the bottom of your feet, are sensitive to pressure or stretching sensations. Receptors in the neck can tell the brain which way the head is turned, and receptors in the ankles can tell the brain how the body is moving relative to the ground.

Proprioception helps a person walk up stairs without looking at each step, to land safely after being thrown unexpectedly, and to sweep an opponent's feet without seeing them. Proprioception cues are perceived much quicker than vision, but both can be tricked. If you make an opponent think you are throwing to the rear, you may be able to launch a forward attack that they are not ready for.

Keeping your physical balance is only a first step. A balanced mental state is best suited for maintaining your physical balance so managing a calm and focused state of mind is also of great importance so that you can be aware of, and freely act on, the cues your body is giving you. The study of balance should then be extended beyond your own body to incorporate methods of disrupting the mental and physical balance of an attacker or opponent (*kuzushi*). Understanding balance and feeling the power such equilibrium brings will ultimately result in seeking a natural balance in your life through continuous improvement.

Leverage

A small amount of force can have a greater effect with the use of leverage. Leverage applies to all techniques in judo, and is particularly useful when your opponent is too heavy to lift with your strength alone.

When you want to lift a heavy stone by yourself, you need a tool like a strong shovel to get a mechanical advantage. If you put the shovel under the stone and push down on the other end,

To improve a throw using leverage, be aware that your grips can lengthen the lever. To maximize your leverage for a throw, grip high on the judogi and place your fulcrum as low as possible.

(*ashiwaza*), hip (*koshiwaza*), shoulder (*tewaza*), or falling body (*sutemiwaza*). Let's look at *ogoshi* as an example. Once *uke* is off balance forward from your *kuzushi*, you merely have to squat low in front of him so your own hips act as a fulcrum. Then, since his upper body is heavier than his lower body, you utilize his own upper body weight to topple him with a relatively small amount of strength. Like a heavy weight added on a balanced scale, that side goes down fast.

Psychology

Psychological principles are also at work in judo. They can help provide an understanding of your opponent's response times under various conditions, the predictability of your opponent's reactions to your attacks or other stimuli, the effect of your own mental state on performance, proven observation and concentration techniques, ways to mentally unbalance your opponent, how to select the optimal timing for an attack, and so on.

If you are successful in instilling fear, uncertainty or doubt in your opponent, this will certainly improve your ability to attack freely. Likewise, you will need to maintain a strong sense of confidence if you are to prevent your opponent from creating doubts in your own mind. After learning some of the physical techniques, an awareness of the mental aspects of judo becomes important if you are to progress and succeed in competition.

Even before the scientific method or the field of psychology was created, fighters were aware of the importance of psychological factors on the outcome of battles. One of the earliest studies of combat is *The Art of War* by Sun Tsu. Written over 2,000 years ago, it lists dangerous character faults that may affect the result of a battle.

- First is recklessness, which leads to destruction. Bravery without forethought causes one to attack blindly and desperately.
- Second is cowardice, which leads to inaction. Timidity can cause one to fail to advance and seize an advantage, or to be too quick to flee from danger.
- Third is a hasty temper, which can be provoked to create vulnerability.

the shovel will act as a long lever. The effort you use multiplied by the distance from the point of support (fulcrum) is equal to the amount of resistance (the weight) you can lift multiplied by its distance from the fulcrum. The mechanical advantage of the lever is determined by dividing the resistance (from the opponent's weight or strength) by the effort you use on the other end of the lever. The longer the shovel is, the greater the leverage you attain to apply force to a heavy object.

Leverage is the reason why a heavy person on a seesaw can be lifted by a lighter person if the lighter person sits further away from the fulcrum than the heavy person. Most judo techniques utilize leverage to multiply your effort to throw, pin, choke, or armlock. Leverage is so basic to judo we seldom think about how much it helps when escaping from a wrist grab, getting a good *tomoenage*, or applying a front cross choke like *nami juji jime*.

In a throw, the objective of your *kuzushi* is to move your opponent's center of gravity off their base before you try to throw *uke* over your leg

Controlling your weaknesses, such as temper, is an essential first step to improving your psychological readiness. Your mental state of readiness can also be affected by your breathing, visual focus, posture, level of distraction, and other factors that can be read and manipulated by a skilled opponent to create opportunities for an attack when you are least able to defend.

It is said that it would require ten years of practice to win victory over one's self and twenty years to win victory over others. Only by cultivating a receptive state of mind, without preconceived ideas or thoughts, can one master the secret art of reacting spontaneously and naturally without hesitation and without purposeless resistance.

Jigoro Kano provided the following advice:

> *The relationship between mind and body is inseparable. The body affects the mind, and the body is also subject to the influences of the mind. It is akin to a shadow following the movements of the object that casts it. Thus, if the spirit is modest, peaceable and correct, this will manifest in one's physical carriage with a posture that demonstrates a certain presence of tranquil solemnity. If the body is unkempt and irregular, the mind will naturally follow to carelessness and self-indulgence. When pondered according to this reasoning, it becomes clear that a man's disposition can be ascertained by examining his posture and manner.*

To succeed in judo *randori* or competition, students learn to control themselves first and foremost, including the psychological aspects of high performance. Work is required on facets of ourselves such as motivation, self-confidence, attention, stress, and control of the level of activation (effort). They can lead us to peak performance, and the best version of ourselves.

Control

As you are learning to control your own body, mind and spirit, also study how to manipulate these in your opponent to gain an advantage. Control of your opponent means your ability to redirect your opponent, whether it is to make an attack or protect yourself in defense. Control

> *"The mind, if slackened even a little, will cause defeat, the same as fearing the opponent will make you unable to use full strength."*
>
> – Kyuzo Mifune, 1883-1965

involves both physical and psychological aspects that can help you perform with consistency and accuracy. It also involves ways to read your opponent and affect their physical and mental state of balance.

Consistency requires technical excellence and precise application of well-coordinated techniques in both offense and defense. Accuracy means your techniques achieve a high percentage of success. This kind of control requires dominating your opponent so that when you attack, he cannot affect the outcome. When your preparation comes together at the right time, you don't miss the *ippon*.

The principle of specificity requires that training conditions be as close as possible to actual competition in order to maximize the effect of the training. For the training to produce the desired results, drills such as *nagekomi* should allow the necessary skills to be repeated safely and in their entirety, while being realistic and reflecting the conditions under which the acquired skills will be used. After developing consistency in your attacks, *randori* is the primary practice method to gain precise, accurate application. You can apply your technique at the right time when *uke* is vulnerable and follow through to prevent *uke* from escaping no matter what he does.

Start with careful observation of the best time to attack. You will soon see ways to take advantage of your opponent's natural movement and to influence his actions to your benefit. Look for weaknesses that can be manipulated, and strengths that can be turned into weaknesses. You want to always be in a position where you are ready to initiate a technique as soon as you spot the opportunity. But even the fastest person can be too late unless you know what your opponent will do before it happens. If someone moves left one step it may be likely that he will take a second

You progress not through what has been done, but by reaching toward what has yet to be done. It is by what you do today that you succeed tomorrow. Such is the virtue of practice.

step in the same direction, especially if you encourage him with a pull. Many people move a certain way time and again. They might move due to natural reactions, training, rhythms, habits, fears, or because you lead them there. These movements can be considered automatic, or at least likely to happen again. This makes them predictable and it becomes possible to anticipate and take advantage of such movements. Through careful observation you can recognize not just where your opponent is, but where he is going.

Control should apply to everything you do in a match. From the moment it begins, control yourself so you are aware, calm, balanced, and relaxed. Then begin asserting your dominating spirit, developing a favorable pace and rhythm, getting your ideal grip, confusing or surprising your opponent, creating or anticipating vulnerabilities, and applying *kuzushi*. Then, when the fleeting opportunity arises, you can complete the attack that your training has prepared you for and which you can do most consistently and accurately.

Maximum effect with minimum effort
(seiryoku zen'yo)

After examining the principles affecting performance in judo, Jigoro Kano formulated one overriding principle that defines good technique. This innovation separated judo from all previous martial arts, and has been adopted by most sports training programs today. Often called the maximum efficiency principle, or *seiryoku zen'yo*, it states that the goal of judo technique is to obtain the greatest possible result for the amount of energy invested.

Learn proper technique so that you can use your energy in the most efficient way.

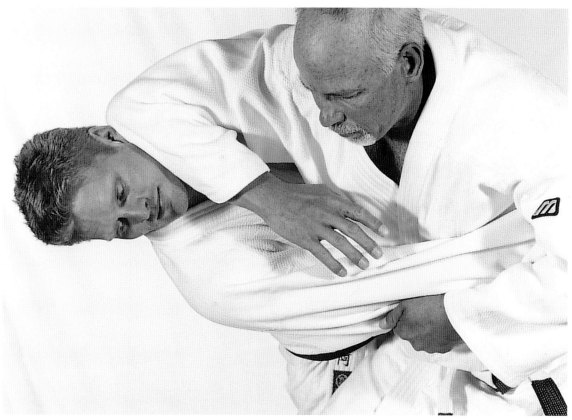

Strikes may be combined with throws to increase effectiveness when necessary to control a threat in a self-defense situation.

Achieving maximum effect with minimum effort requires just the right amount of force to be exerted to accomplish the desired result. Too little is not ideal, nor is too much. One common misunderstanding of this principle is that the use of strength or force is always negative. Certainly, misapplication, unnecessary use or excessive use of strength in a way that wastes energy is not desirable. But considerable strength may be essential, even when applied correctly, against a large or strong opponent of equal skill. Technique will overcome strength or size, but the larger the imbalance in size or strength, the greater your skill level will have to be relative to your opponent.

The physical education aspects of judo ensure the development of a strong, well-coordinated body, but most top athletes today supplement judo practice with strength training. This is because the development of power improves competitive performance and is a critical component of technique. Naturally, power must be applied correctly in accord with proper leverage and biomechanics. The goal is the maximum efficient use of power, or the best use of energy.

One key aspect of this principle is the concept of *kuzushi*, or breaking balance. The idea is that you can maximize the result of any attack on an opponent whose balance is broken, whereas an opponent who retains control of his or her balance can easily move or resist successfully. The careful study of *kuzushi* is perhaps the most important element of learning successful throwing and grappling skills.

Flexibility and adaptability are also key components of judo. Your arms should be strong like chains, but loose enough to bend at a moment's notice. Similarly, your legs should be powerful, but able to move with lightning speed. And finally, your mental state must be determined, yet relaxed enough to change direction. This is the essence of judo – the right application of strength, at the right time and in the right place.

CHAPTER 5:
HOW JUDO DEVELOPS CHARACTER

Judo is much more than just physical training; it is essentially a way to develop the mind and body so they can work harmoniously together. The emphasis in class is always on the physical aspects, but there are additional benefits in terms of developing a strong and healthy character. The struggle of judo training refines the self, but also benefits others. Offering yourself to your training partner requires complete trust and engenders mutual respect. Even top international competitors train together to become better. Honing their own skills, they help their rivals to improve.

The moral and ethical underpinnings of judo, inherited partly from Japanese warrior tradition, provide a way to consider judo as a larger activity than what takes place on the mat.

The principles of judo are multi-dimensional: they apply not only to physical skills, but to other parts of life too. When you maximize your efforts, you are practicing judo. Developing your character and striving to improve is a way of practicing judo. Exhibiting courage in the face of adversity is judo. Working for the welfare of others and contributing to the betterment of the world is the ultimate way of practicing judo.

Mental approach to training

Judo cultivates, even requires, a positive can-do attitude. Practice will reinforce the understanding that results come from personal effort, and that great achievements can be made with enough determination. A step-by-step approach to mastering the physical skills gradually builds character traits that will make you successful in other areas of life as well. Since the purpose of judo is to subdue an opponent, it is vital to approach it with a serious attitude. Take your training seriously at all times for safety and maximum benefit.

The laws of nature must be fully experienced to be understood; they cannot be bent to the preconceived ideas of the observer. To master judo you must move in a natural manner, which means surrendering yourself to the way things are, rather than the way you would like them to be. This discovery of the natural principles of judo must be an intensely personal revelation achieved through intense training. Only when you apply yourself wholeheartedly to the training will you gain glimpses of meaning and higher principles. As Jigoro Kano wrote, "If there is effort, there is always accomplishment."

It is not uncommon for students to consider giving up practice because of lack of success in competition, unavailability of practice partners, a perceived lack of progress, injury, personal problems outside of class, or other concerns. These are simply additional obstacles to overcome in learning judo and developing self-discipline. Setting goals is often helpful, whether it is for proficiency in a particular technique, achieving a black belt rank or defeating an opponent in competition. The successful student is one who climbs over, moves around or knocks down each barrier. Of course, in conformance with the meaning of *ju* (flexibility), no set course of action will work against every obstacle.

Character lessons

There are lessons to be learned in studying most physical activities. When the lessons in judo are applied to everyday living, they help to elevate our life experience. Such lessons include discipline, perseverance, loyalty, the importance of flexibility in our approach to problems, understanding the relationship between success and efforts expended, and working through the process of training to achieve excellence.

Jigoro Kano's Moral Code for Judo

Courtesy: be polite to others

Courage: bravely face difficulties

Friendship: be a considerate and reliable friend

Honesty: be sincere with your thoughts and actions

Honor: do what is right and stand by your principles

Modesty: show humility and act without ego

Respect: appreciate and honor others

Self-control: show restraint, maintain disciplined behavior

With no team to rely on or hold you back, judo is more of an individual achievement than many other sporting activities. It is hard to blame others or to get undeserved credit in judo. This leads to a sense of personal responsibility for your actions. It does not mean that others cannot push you to greater heights (or steer you in the wrong direction), but in judo your performance is a direct result of your own ability, preparation and fighting spirit. You cannot use equipment to gain an advantage, and there is nothing to hide behind when you fail; it is a face-to-face form of combat that shapes character.

Beginners often think judo experts are tough – and they are right. However, to beginners this means that they can dish out punishment at will and never be defeated. In popular culture, the toughest martial artist is the one who can beat up all the others, but this represents a misconception about the toughness that judo engenders. The truth is quite the opposite. The toughness of a judo expert is a direct result of perseverance through harsh trials. It is better measured by the punishment you can take than by the punishment you can give. One value in judo training is the opportunity to test yourself and push yourself to your limits, continually expanding your limits and extending your capabilities.

Judo is a science implying mastery of various laws of nature, but it is also an art. The true value of any art form – whether judo, music or sculpture – is its goal of discovering and developing the artist's true potential. Judo is a method of self-realization and expression. Its fundamental techniques, practice methods, philosophy and moral basis are consistent with the free pursuit of insights into the self and the development of a strong individual character.

With even a little introspection, you will see the benefits of training in attack and defense. The qualities you will master include patience, perseverance, optimism, dependability, honesty, thoughtfulness, adaptability, independence, humility, courage, discipline, self-reliance, intensity, sincerity, resilience and cooperation. Other traits developed through judo are self-respect, deliberation, kindness, composure and self-control. All of this can be summed up by one of the goals of judo practice: *jika no kansei*, or to strive for perfection as a whole person.

Mutual welfare and benefit (jita kyoei)

Judo is about more than personal development. If your focus is always on yourself you will grow out of balance and become selfish. Jigoro Kano realized that achieving personal excellence depends to a great extent on others. For this reason he adopted the maxim *jita kyoei* to express his belief that your self-development cannot be at the expense of others since the objective of self-development is to contribute something of value to the world. *Jita kyoei* is often translated as "mutual welfare and benefit," but more literally means "you and I shining together," or "mutual prosperity for self and others." All practice must be in conformance with this tenet of judo.

It goes without saying that the reckless study of attack and defense can result in injury. When you practice with a partner you are giving him your body and relying on him to take care of you. This requires a level of dependence and trust that cannot be achieved without genuine caring about your partner. Ideally, every form of judo practice has a benefit for both parties. Even while someone is practicing techniques on you, your attention should be focused on learning the aspects of the attacks that are most effective for your own use, as well as the weaknesses that can be exploited to counter attack.

Learning to hold an opponent down and learning to escape from the hold are the opposite sides of the same technique. Learning how to fall for each throw is an essential step in learning how to perform the throws. Most people learn lessons by initially losing in tournaments, but gradually

> *It may well be said that the primary objective of practicing judo is perfection of character*
> – H Seichiro Okazaki

go on to win. Like both ends of a circle, you and your training partner are linked together into a whole, and we all depend on others to try their best so we can improve. This leads to a greater understanding of our interconnectedness and social responsibility.

In judo we seek the state of equilibrium that is called balance. In a dynamic world this harmony can never be achieved in isolation; you must learn how to work with other people. By studying the art of attack and defense you learn to resolve conflicts and contribute to peace.

Even as a newborn baby gasps its first precious breath, it learns it is on its own. Although it is totally dependent on others, the infant believes that it must fight for survival. In judo, too, we rely on others to show us the way, but each student must have the will to fight. Progress comes primarily as a result of individual effort, but is best achieved when we are challenged and assisted by others. Developing our strength, intellect and morality ultimately has little value unless used in a positive way to benefit society. Just as a baby begins teaching others about life as soon as it is born, even though it struggles to learn the most basic things, we all have something to give, and we all have something to learn from others.

Recognize that the real battle is inside yourself.

CHAPTER 6:
CLASSIFICATION OF TECHNIQUES
(waza)

Waza refers to the methods used to overcome greater strength and size with a high degree of technical skill, timing and agility. It is a supreme compliment when your *sensei* tells you that your *waza* is good.

It is important to learn a variety of techniques so you will be prepared to take advantage of any opportunity. Most competitors develop favorite techniques, or *tokui waza*, to a point that they can be applied with confidence against any type of opponent. But even favorite techniques often rely on strategies to encourage or force the opponent into a vulnerable position for the attack. Other attacks, at least the threat of other attacks, are used to set up the opponent so your favorite throw, pin, choke, or armlock will work. The larger your arsenal of techniques, the more opportunities you will be able to create on your feet and on the ground.

There are three main types of *waza* (techniques):

- All throws used to get an opponent to the ground with force;
- Grappling techniques – usually (not always) used on the ground;
- Striking techniques used only for self-defense.

Throwing (nage waza)

There are 68 basic throwing techniques defined by the Kodokan. The *gokyo no waza* (five groups of technique) is the standard syllabus of judo throws originated by the founder of judo in 1895 at the Kodokan. Since 1920 the Kodokan *gokyo no waza* has been comprised of 40 throws in five numbered groups.

On the 100th anniversary of the Kodokan in 1982, an additional eight traditional judo throws that had been taken out of the *gokyo no waza* in 1920 were reinstated, and 17 new techniques were recognized as official Kodokan Judo throws collectively called *shinmeisho no waza*. In 1997 the Kodokan added two more throws. Twenty years later, in 2017, the Kodokan added two additional throws and removed one technique (*daki age*) that was considered dangerous and prohibited in competition. The 68 throwing techniques currently recognized by the Kodokan are shown in Appendix 1.

Standard throwing techniques are divided into *waza* executed from a standing position (*tachi waza*) and sacrifice techniques executed while falling down (*sutemi waza*). There are three types of standing techniques, depending on the primary part of the body used to make the throw: hip throws (*koshi waza*), hand or arm throws (*te waza*) and foot or leg throws (*ashi waza*). Sacrifice throws are divided into those to the rear (*ma sutemi waza*) and those to the side (*yoko sutemi waza*).

These classifications describe the main element that makes a throw work in its classic form, but when techniques are performed differently from the traditional version, they may not appear consistent with the category in which they are classified. There are an almost infinite number of variations of techniques that are not easily classified. Many throws have been modified, or specialized variations created specifically for modern competition. For example, the shoulder wheel (*kata guruma*) is recognized as a hand throw (*te waza*), but was modified for competition and performed as a sacrifice throw, yet it is still commonly referred to as *kata guruma* because of the recognizable throwing action of wheeling your opponent over your shoulder. Likewise, *uchi mata* is a leg throw but may be performed as much more of a hip throw.

The Kodokan taxonomy of judo provides a framework for understanding and learning throwing techniques by grouping them according to the general part of the body which is most essential to the performance of the throw, but it should not be viewed as a restriction that prevents you from completing a throw in *randori* even if it varies from the traditional method. Variations of throws are numerous and important because they can be very effective, but understanding the naming structure ensures that students and teachers can communicate the basic skills in a relatively consistent manner.

Grappling (katame waza)

Grappling techniques are methods of controlling opponents so they are forced to submit and cooperate because they are immobilized, threatened with injury or rendered unconscious. Grappling techniques can be expected to end a match or confrontation conclusively. They involve the closest possible range of combat where other techniques are less effective.

When grappling techniques are performed on the ground they are called *newaza*. Many can also be executed while standing, or used to force an opponent onto the ground. *Katame waza* is divided into pinning techniques (*osaekomi waza*), strangulations or choking techniques (*shime waza*) and joint locks (*kansetsu waza*). All can be used to force submission in different ways.

Osaekomi waza involves pinning your opponent to the ground so he or she cannot get away, whereas you are free to escape if desired. Judo pins control your opponent so that he is helpless and vulnerable with his back on the ground (in the judo *kata,* self-defense training, and when applying submissions, there are also times when your opponent is held face down).

Shime waza includes chokes and strangles applied with the arms, legs, or *judogi*. Your opponent can be quickly rendered unconscious with a properly applied strangle. Often the more he resists, the more quickly the strangle works.

Although *kansetsu waza* includes any kind of joint lock (even neck or spine locks), only joint locks to the elbow are allowed in free practice or competition today because of the increased risk of injury when using locks to other joints. Other joint locks (such as knee, wrist and finger locks) are still practiced in judo, usually by more advanced students, as part of various *kata*.

The Kodokan recognizes 32 *katame waza* techniques: 10 *osaekomi waza*, 12 *shime waza* and 10 *kansetsu waza* (see Appendix 2).

Striking *(atemi waza)*

Striking techniques are used in order to disable, distract or unbalance your opponent in self-defense, but are not permitted in modern judo competition or *randori*. For safety they are usually practiced in *kata* form and are considered specialized techniques for study after attaining black belt. As they are seldom practiced in judo classes or required for promotion, they are not demonstrated in this book.

Striking is a long-range fighting skill. Judo strategy calls for closing the distance and gaining control over your opponent. The closer your opponent is, the more difficult it is to make a powerful strike and the less important striking skills are. *Atemi waza* are often used to make the transition to a close-contact range of fighting so you can use throws, submissions or control holds.

Strikes may be used to distract and break an opponent's balance, then combined with other techniques, such as throws. They are equally effective on the ground to weaken an opponent's defenses and set up a more conclusive joint lock, submission or control hold.

Striking skills are divided into arm and hand strikes (*ude waza*) and foot or knee strikes (*ashi ate*). Sometimes the head may be used. Common strikes include punches, kicks, knee and elbow strikes, chops and jabs.

Specific vital points are used as targets. Many are pressure points or sensitive areas that result in greater pain when struck. Some strikes can cause permanent damage. Certain strikes to the throat, eyes, bridge of the nose, kidneys, knees and groin, for instance, can severely injure an opponent and are never practiced with full force contact.

Practicing different types of techniques permits an appropriate level of response to control any threat.

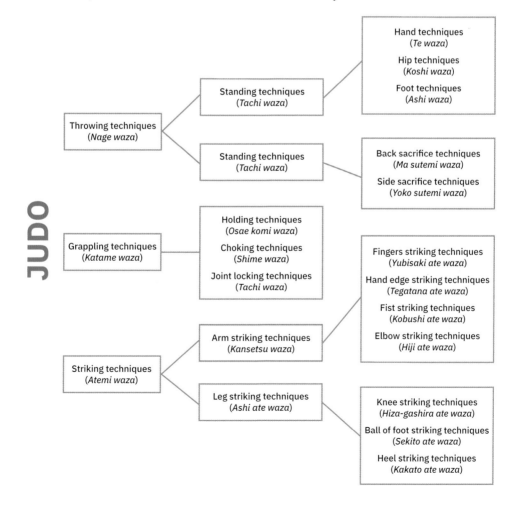

CHAPTER 1:
PRINCIPLES OF THROWING

Judo is not just a random collection of techniques. Progress comes from a real understanding, physically and mentally, of the principles involved in the various actions. A principle is a natural law or essential element of judo technique that is part of its intrinsic nature and transcends a specific trained movement. Once learned, you can use the principle to solve problems you have not faced before.

You can learn a wide variety of meaningful fighting principles by studying judo. Examples are the important elements of combat range or engagement distance (*maai*), proper technique (*waza*) and combat awareness (*zanshin*). These principles involve combat theories best learned from a standing position, although they apply equally when on the ground with an opponent.

All judo matches start standing. Keeping your own balance is a vital first step to protect yourself or get away from an attack. The next step, unbalancing your opponent, requires skill in gripping, posture, movement and control. Once learned, the art of throwing will enable you to take advantage of a momentary lapse in balance to render a dangerous opponent helpless. This chapter discusses the basic skills you need to become an expert at *nage waza*.

Gripping (kumikata)

Top competitors understand how to dominate opponents and distract them from their match strategy. An important objective in combat is to bring the opponent into your area of relative strength, to fight on your terms. One way of doing this is through superior gripping skills. A contestant with a superior grip can attack freely, while preventing the opponent from doing so. Strike like a hawk, clench your opponent, then take him airborne, or at least maintain the dominant grip to constrict your prey's movements.

In judo competition, or in a conflict off the mat, it is vital to control the space between you and your opponent. This is the area you have to maneuver through to get into a close attack position – and your opponent has to travel through this same space to attack you. The primary tool you have to control that space is your grip.

Another purpose of gripping skill, or *kumikata*, is to provide the turning leverage usually needed to unbalance and throw an opponent. Grips along the opponent's center line are generally considered more defensive, whereas wider grips permit more attacks. For this reason, the most standard grip is one hand on the lapel at the chest and the other hand on the sleeve. This gives a balanced grip for optimal attack and defense. The pulling hand on the sleeve is called *hikite*, and the lifting or power hand at the lapel is called *tsurite*. Practice your

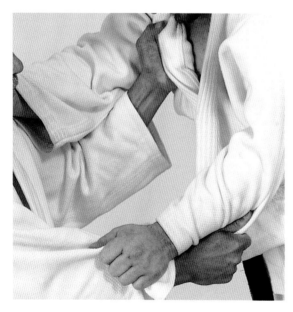

The left versus right grip is known as *kenka yotsu*.

"Judo is the only martial art derived from jujutsu where the grip of the opponent is obligatory; this is what gave its technical wealth, finesse and intelligence."

– IJF Rules, 2022

attacks from different grips so you will be prepared to throw even when your favorite grip is not possible.

Kumikata provides the physical connection with your opponent that allows you to feel and anticipate an attack before it becomes a real threat. Because judo is a close-range form of fighting, reaction time must be extremely fast and visual cues are not very useful. You must learn to react to tactile stimuli, and your reactions must become reflexive. With training, your grip can give you valuable information about your opponent's actions early enough for you to respond. In addition to helping with your defense, your hands help you recognize when your opponent is in a vulnerable position so you can best apply your own throws. To gain these benefits, your arms must be relaxed so you can perceive subtle shifts in movement and balance. It is normal to try to throw your opponent after his balance is broken, but it is better to feel the opponent's intentions, anticipate his movements, and apply the throw as his balance is broken.

In today's high-level competition, gripping skills have become a vital component of success. Tournament rules relating to how you can grip your opponent when standing are intended to prevent defensive play and to ensure a fair fight. You may not avoid gripping in order to prevent action. Learn to use the grip that maximizes your ability to throw, while allowing you to defend against dominant grips from your opponent.

The most important rule is that you cannot grab below the belt (except in *newaza*). The 2022 IJF Rules state that you can take a variety of grips as long as you are attacking:

> *"Collar and lapel, one side, cross grip, belt grip, pocket and pistol grips are allowed when the attitude of the judoka is positive, when they are looking to perform positive attacks and throws."*

As you train for your favorite throws, you must prepare for two fundamental forms of *kumikata*. *Aiyotsu* is when both contestants take the same right- or left-handed grip (e.g. they both have their right hand on the opponent's lapel). *Kenka yotsu* is the non-symmetrical grip when a left-handed fighter meets a right-handed fighter (e.g. one grabs the lapel with his left hand while the other grabs the lapel with his right hand).

Posture *(shisei)*

In many sports, a defensive posture is characterized by a low, bent-over position, while offensive posture is more upright. An offensive player with a football or basketball generally moves or stands with slightly bent legs while looking for an opportunity. The opposing defender has legs spread farther apart, assumes a more crouched position. If a defender gets the ball he stands up straighter to take the offense because the standing position gives freedom of movement to change directions, use either foot, deceive opponents with feints, and see the entire competition area.

In judo you cannot win without an effective attack, so the emphasis in practice is on the correct offensive posture. Even in defense, a judoka is always looking to move swiftly into attack which is more difficult without good posture.

The ideal posture to freely apply judo throws is an upright natural posture, with knees slightly bent, head centered over the hips, feet directly below the hips and about shoulder width apart. Position your head so you look not down at your feet, but up around your opponent's waist or above. Movement of the hips will usually signal your opponent's real intentions better than his or her feet or hands, which often are used deceptively.

The ideal judo posture allows for free movement, and is inherently stable and balanced. The upright natural posture gives the best overall view of the field of battle, prevents you from being dominated, and allows you maximum freedom to react spontaneously when needed. The rules of competition penalize an overly defensive, bent-over position because it inhibits action. In *randori* you also want to maximize opportunities which is easier to do with the correct posture.

The perfect technique is one without much effort or conscious thought, applied at the right time, in the right direction, with the right

Good balance requires good posture.

amount of force – a spontaneous reaction to the opportunity presented by the opponent's movement, grip, posture, or momentary lapse in defense. This perfection is rare.

In fact, technique is like water forever slipping through our fingers; we can only hope to cup our hands and capture some of it. We can seize it for a moment, sometimes long enough to take a refreshing drink, but it is too fluid to capture at will. The natural posture is therefore essential for the quick responses needed to take advantage of fleeting opportunities.

Movement *(tai sabaki and shintai)*

Since judo requires you to maintain your own balance even in the face of a skilled opponent who is trying to knock you down, how you move your feet and your body is important. *Shintai* refers to the methods of moving used in judo.

The most useful method is *tsugi ashi*, which is often used in practice, particularly while learning certain throws or when entering for an attack. In *tsugi ashi* (literally 'next' or 'following foot') one foot always leads and the other always follows without bringing them completely together. You may be moving forward, backwards or to the side. *Ayumi ashi* is normal walking where each foot moves in front of the other.

In both cases, the feet should slide on the mat when stepping, with little or no lifting in order to maintain constant contact with the ground. This sliding style of stepping is called *suri ashi* which is intended to make it more difficult for an opponent to catch you on one foot, to permit you to push off the ground at any moment to apply an attack, and to give you greater stability while moving.

In tournaments or free practice your foot movements are crucial to maintaining a stable position. The easiest way for an opponent to throw you is to attack when you move your feet before your body, or when you move them in an attempt to catch up with your body. Learn to keep your feet directly under your hips as much

Success is going from failure to failure without losing your enthusiasm.

– Winston Churchill

as possible. Crossing your feet, lifting them up, bringing them together or separating them too much can all lead to being thrown. At the same time, being too predictable in your movement is dangerous too.

Knowledge of balance is the secret that enables masters of judo to throw stronger and heavier assailants without any great effort. It is the quick and agile person who has the ability to regain balance more easily, not the big, strong person, for strength is not a factor in balance. How well you move will be the determining factor in any conflict, whether you are strong or weak. To keep your movements natural and agile, avoid tension and rigidity in your body. Suppleness in your movement allows you to attack freely while retaining your balance and responding appropriately to your opponent's initiatives.

Tai sabaki, or body control, is the method of turning used to defend yourself from throws, and to set up or enter for an attack of your own. The concept of *tai sabaki* is that the fluid movement

of the body, particularly the rotation of the body when it is upright, creates forces that can be used to help you evade throws, block throws or effect throws. For example, by rotating your body in a small arc while holding your opponent, you can make your opponent move in a much larger arc around you. This allows you to maintain your own balance while you take advantage of your opponent's greater movement.

Unbalancing *(kuzushi)*

The sense of balance is often taken for granted by athletes, overlooked as a skill worthy of study. But mastery of balance is compulsory to develop fighting skills. Jigoro Kano emphasized it as the key to success in judo.

Balance is controlled by a combination of three sensory inputs: the vestibular system in the inner ear, vision and proprioception. Most people focus on vision as the primary tool to maintain balance, but proprioception is more vital in judo. This is the kinesthetic perception of movement and spatial orientation arising from stimuli within the body itself. It is often more reliable than vision, and is the feel you get only from repeated practice. Balance involves a delicate interplay between forces to achieve a state of equilibrium or, conversely, a state of imbalance. The subtlety of your opponent's balance can often be detected only through your hands, which are in contact with your opponent.

Sometimes judo students are frustrated when they cannot easily apply throws on skilled training partners. As you progress, keep in mind that students who practice judo are probably the hardest people in the world to knock off their feet because they learn through painful experience what will befall them if they lose their balance. They become expert in ways to retain control of their balance, or to regain it when it is in danger of being lost.

Although simple to understand in concept, *kuzushi* is difficult to achieve against a trained opponent who is conscious of his balance, who maintains good posture, and moves quickly with confidence. Against an attacker untrained in judo, the secrets of *kuzushi* will usually work easily to weaken his position so that he can be defeated.

Kuzushi literally means 'to destroy, demolish or break down'. In judo it means to unbalance your opponent, or to break his posture and destroy his stability. Its purpose is to bring your opponent into a vulnerable position, one in which he or she cannot defend successfully. This can be a dynamic disruption of your opponent's balance, or it can be simply adapting to your opponent's movement. *Kuzushi* is attained when your opponent's center of gravity is not directly over his feet.

Sometimes *kuzushi* is applied directly by simply pushing or pulling, which is how it is initially practiced as you are learning throws. Each hand has a specific role in bringing your opponent in the desired direction. The pushing or pulling motion is an integral part of each throw that must be strengthened and coordinated. You may eventually find that your own strength is sometimes insufficient to force your opponent's weight into a vulnerable position, and that your opponent can use his own muscles and mass to fight back.

Another way of directly applying *kuzushi* is by generating momentum from moving your body, then using this force to disrupt the balance of your opponent. Do this by moving your body quickly in the direction of the desired throw, building momentum the faster you move. Then transfer that momentum to your opponent's body when you bump into him (moving forward), or reach the limit of your arm length (moving back). This sudden transfer of momentum can result in a large, and relatively effortless, unbalancing force.

Because judo is a fluid activity with both contestants moving constantly, there are many opportunities for you to create and take advantage of momentary lapses in balance while shifting weight between the feet. *Kuzushi* achieved from one attempted throw can be used to attack with another follow-up throw. This is the basis for combination techniques that use the initial attack as a form of *kuzushi*. Alternatively, the shifting

There are three primary ways of applying *kuzushi*:

- your direct action
  (e.g. pulling or pushing as you enter for a throw);
- inducing your opponent's action
  (e.g. a feint or combination attack);
- direct action by your opponent
  (e.g. a counter throw).

state of balance during your opponents' attacks can be used against them, and they can be thrown with counter throws.

How should you deal with someone who attempts to pull you forward into a throw? If you resist by pulling back you may be thrown in that direction, but if you go forwards you may be in danger of falling right into a forward throw. The answer is to use the attacker's pull to throw him while keeping your own balance.

To do this you can step forward faster and stronger than his pull required, so that you seize the initiative and unbalance him. By adding your own power and momentum to his pulling action, you can throw your opponent backwards with twice the force. A safer option is to step diagonally forward and to one side, so that you go with the pull but redirect it into a new direction that forces the attacker off balance, preventing him from throwing you in the direction he was pulling.

As you become more advanced you learn to use your opponents' own efforts against them. Your opponent's strength can only be applied to you to the degree that you try to resist it. Without resistance, strength is meaningless. The idea is that you push when pulled, and pull when pushed – one way of yielding, the meaning of *ju*.

An opponent's movement can help you apply *kuzushi* in other ways to achieve the state of imbalance that sets up a throw. If your opponent is moving forward, for example, and you stop his feet from moving while continuing the momentum of the upper body, his center of gravity will naturally extend out in front of his feet so he can be toppled easily. An example of this type of *kuzushi* is seen in the throw *sasae tsurikomi ashi*.

Alternatively, if you simply stop or prevent the motion of your opponent's upper body while he is initiating a quick movement forward, he may complete the step he started and leave his center of gravity behind him so that you can throw him backwards with a throw such as *osoto gari*.

To create this kind of imbalance all you have to do is get the feet to move at a different speed than

the upper body – either faster or slower. Since you can partially control the movement of the upper body through proper gripping (*kumikata*), you can influence your opponent's balance in almost undetectable ways as he moves his feet. You can also make him move his feet away from his center of gravity by applying foot sweeps, or making other attacks that cause him to move his feet, while controlling his upper body.

Another type of *kuzushi* based on the scientific principle of action-reaction is called *hando no kuzushi*, or reactionary breaking of balance. Using this principle you apply force to the opponent, but when you feel the typical response of resistance you reverse the direction to take advantage of the opponent's reaction. In this way every action or reaction of the opponent can be turned against him. Through constant practice you can anticipate certain reactions to your pushing or pulling, and then put yourself into a position to seize the opportunity you created through your action. Resistance often leads to defeat and it is sometimes better to resist with non-resistance.

To visualize the objective of *kuzushi*, imagine a large box representing an opponent (see diagram). While the box can be pushed backward or to one side (and many throws do exactly that), it is weakest when perched on one corner. This is the state often sought in judo so that a throw can be applied with the least amount of effort and strength. In this position the balance of the box is so precarious that it can be thrown in nearly any direction. In the case of a person who might try to move, this position also places all of his weight

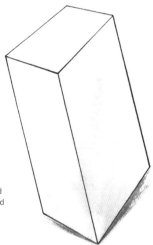

Think of this box as an opponent. It can be pushed backward or to one side and is weakest when perched on one corner. That is the principle of *kuzushi*.

Learn to maintain a calm inner centre in order to be able to weather the storm around you.

your true objective. Gripping is very important as a means for controlling your opponent's focus of attention, as well as his posture and balance.

You can also sometimes create a mindset that can be used to defeat your opponent. For example, you can keep your opponent so mentally occupied in defending your attacks that he finds it difficult to initiate his own attacks. Certain attacks may be used simply to lure your opponent into a particular desired reaction. By constantly attacking with backward throws, you can create an almost unconscious reaction in your opponent, forcing him to maintain a posture with a slight forward push. Since the mind controls the body, you can often only apply *kuzushi* to an opponent who does not realize you are doing it.

Mastering *kuzushi* also means mentally training to prevent a sudden crisis from destroying your own demeanor. Judo training will help you to develop healthy reactions to a variety of confrontations. You will also develop a strong spirit, so that you can endure people who try to intimidate or bully you, while remaining focused on your own specific objectives. Learning how to control your emotional reaction and rely on a calm inner self are part of maintaining the state of harmony that is balance.

Judo fundamentally revolves around the principle of balance. In fact, all things in life seek the balanced state, which is simply the unity of opposites. Life is the constant effort to elevate yourself while achieving and maintaining the harmonious state of balance from which you cannot fall. There can be no better training for this kind of life than judo.

Fitting in *(tsukuri)*

A vital component of every throw is getting into the position needed to best apply the technique with minimal effort. Fitting in for the throw is called *tsukuri* (literally 'to make'). It is closely linked with methods of *tai sabaki* and *kuzushi*, which often happen at the same time you are entering for a throw. While *kuzushi* is focused on creating your opponent's unbalanced weak position, *tsukuri* is focused on your own balance while putting yourself into a position of strength. The object of *tsukuri* is to maintain your opponent's weak position while aligning your own body to take advantage of the opponent's loss of balance.

onto one part of one foot, making it difficult or impossible to move that foot to escape. Part of the benefit of *kuzushi* is that it often pins the opponent into a vulnerable position from which he cannot regain balance. This requires a finely tuned sense of balance and complete control over the opponent.

There is also a form of mental *kuzushi* used to disturb your opponent psychologically or unbalance his or her composure and concentration. This can be achieved simply with a fighting spirit that dominates your opponent, use of the *kiai* (spirit shout), or physical maneuvers that distract the opponent's attention away from

Tsukuri is the part of a throw practiced repeatedly in *uchikomi* so that the ideal throwing position can be attained quickly and spontaneously on demand. Appropriate emphasis should be made on creating and maintaining proper *kuzushi* during every practice of *tsukuri*. There are standard entries for basic throws, but also many individual variations for different body types, personal preferences, situations and opportunities.

Through repetition you make the technique your own, adapt it to fit your particular preferences, and find out what works against different opponents. Stepping or pivoting into the correct foot position is a critical aspect of *tsukuri*. During these steps you are most vulnerable to a counter attack so they must be fast and accurate. It is especially important to master the rotating action needed for forward throws like *seoi nage*, shoulder throw. To apply this type of throw, you turn to face the same way as your opponent so

he or she can be pulled onto or around your back. These turning actions are called *tai sabaki*, and the core concept is that you must continue breaking your opponent's balance by using the rotating action of your body in conjunction with your pulling. The pulling force should come more from the rotation and momentum of your body than the strength in your arms.

The most basic entry taught to beginners (Method 1 below) is to step forward with the right foot, placing it in front of the left foot, then to pivot on the ball of the right foot as you turn and bring the left foot back in line with the right foot. Method 2 is to begin with the left foot, deceptively stepping in front of your right foot, then spinning in (*mawarikomi*) for the attack to the right side. Method 3, which is particularly fast and strong, is where the left foot steps first, behind the right foot. This type of rotation can be done while stepping backwards, pulling strongly with the left hand as you step away from your opponent to

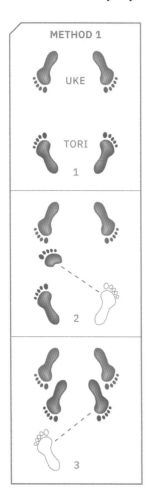

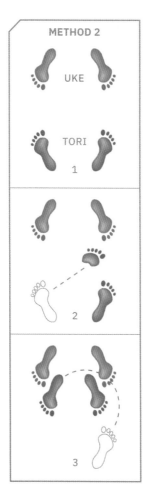

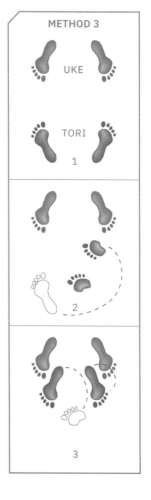

generate forward momentum. It is called drawing out (*hikidashi*). The fastest but most difficult method is to jump in with both feet at the same time as you turn in the air (*tobikomi*).

Turning or stepping to enter for a throw is an important part of *tsukuri*, but other critical elements include the position of your hands on your opponent, the exact alignment of your feet on the mat (or on the opponent), the direction of your push or pull with each hand, your body posture, bending your knees, and the position of your shoulders and head.

Application (kake)

The final phase of any throw is called *kake* – application of the technique. After breaking your opponent's balance so he is in a disadvantageous position (*kuzushi*), move your body into the most advantageous position for applying the technique (*tsukuri*), then execute it (*kake*). Think of *kuzushi* as disrupting an opponent's balance, and *kake* as making the state of imbalance decisive and permanent.

The *kake* in each technique is completed differently. You may bend, twist, sweep, push, fall or roll to finish a throw. Often the application of a technique involves a complex movement of turning while leaning, pulling with the hands and driving with the legs. Coordination of the various parts of the throw is an important skill; the more efficient it is, the more power and control you have.

A critical part of every throw is the follow through. After your opponent starts to fall, you must maintain control and continue to execute the technique, following the opponent to the ground. Many skilled judo competitors can turn out to escape from a throw if given even a minimal loss of contact or control by the thrower. Since the objective in competition is to ensure your opponent falls on his back with force and speed, your control of the opponent must be flawless and continuous until his back hits the ground (and even afterwards, to initiate groundwork while still in an advantageous position). In modern competition this type of approach is called terminal judo, because when the proper angle of attack is utilized with good follow through, every throw will end with both contestants driven onto the mat with force.

Combination techniques
(renraku and renzoku waza)

Judo is not as simple as memorizing the various techniques and how to apply them. If it were that easy, there would be many more black belts. The problem when trying to apply your favorite throw successfully is that your opponent never stands still. As you improve your technique, your opponent is often improving his defenses. This means you may have to force or coax your opponent into a position of vulnerability, and immediately take advantage of the opportunity created.

Before you can expect to be successful with combination techniques you need to master the basic throws and common defenses. However, combinations are essential for intermediate and advanced students, who often have difficulty with single attacks against equally skilled opponents or with defensive opponents who are ready to apply a counter throw.

Any good attempt at a throw should at least make your opponent lose balance and become vulnerable to a subsequent attack. In the fleeting moments while he or she is regaining balance, you should be spontaneously attacking with a combination throw, or *renraku waza*. Naturally, the technique used must be appropriate to the situation. This requires training on transitions between throws, taking into account the likely reactions of your opponent.

When you repeatedly attack with certain throws your opponent's response eventually becomes predictable. Each attempted throw generally results in specific evasions, blocks and counter attacks from your opponent. When you see this happening, it is time to prepare for your opponent's response and continue directly into another attack. Sometimes a string of attacks in the same direction (*renzoku waza*) can force your opponent off balance. Sometimes you need to change the direction of attack (*renraku waza*). Basically, you learn to anticipate the defense and prepare yourself with a response. This is an active form of breaking balance, or *kuzushi*.

One type of combination attack is to continue directly from a throwing attempt into a technique on the ground, such as an arm lock or a pin. A common example is *tai otoshi* (body drop) followed by *juji gatame* (cross arm lock). Once on the ground you should continue to be flexible in your attacks, moving fluidly from one attack to another. Sometimes as your opponent begins to escape from your pin you can switch to another pin, or achieve a submission by choke or arm lock. Yielding to superior strength may lead to other openings, whereas rigidly sticking with a weak position usually leads to defeat.

To succeed with combination techniques, your transition from one throw to another must be seamless and quick. Your training should include practice of combinations for your favorite throws so you can perform them naturally, without thinking. Preparations you make today will help you win tomorrow.

See Chapter 15 and Appendix 4 for more information.

Counter techniques
(kaeshi waza)

When you are attacked, your opponent gives you a present of his strength. You must know how to receive it and turn it to your advantage. Counter techniques, or *kaeshi waza*, rely on an opponent's attack to create the momentum and *kuzushi* for your own attack. Counter techniques are risky in that you must allow your opponent to take the initiative, so they require confidence that you can successfully resist being thrown. Specialists in *kaeshi waza* find, however, that when they are prepared for an attack it is easier to take advantage of an opponent than when he is not moving. Every attempted attack creates certain vulnerabilities that can be exploited – if you can retain your own balance.

The best way to retain your balance and prepare for a counterattack is to spoil the key element that makes your opponent's attempted throw work. To do this, you must thoroughly understand the principles of each throw that you want to counter. You can then react to each throw with the exact movement required to stop it. You can also deceptively create an apparent opportunity for your opponent to attack, knowing that when he does you are ready with a counter. For example, you may leave one foot in front of the other, encouraging your opponent to see it as an opportunity for a foot sweep, while you are prepared to counter the sweep when it comes.

Jigoro Kano recognized three different levels of combative initiative, or sen:

- *Go no sen* is the form of attack we normally think of as a counterattack. By taking advantage of the opponent's movement and position after he or she has started the attack, this form of attack initiative is considered a late form of initiative. It is usually characterized as a defensive response, or counteraction to an unsuccessful attack attempted by your opponent.

- *Sen* is the form of attack initiative that is also defensive, but launched simultaneously with the aggressor's attack. This requires a definitive understanding of the form the attack will take, based on the initial move or preparation leading up to the attack.

- *Sen-sen no sen* is a subconscious form of attack initiative that is also defensive, but appears to be offensive. The aggressor's attack is anticipated and 'beaten to the punch' by an appropriate action. This requires that you should recognize your opponent's intent even before the attack has been launched.

One thing you learn very well in judo is that every attack has an appropriate defense. One of the earliest westerners to witness judo in the 19th century was Lafcadio Hearn, who wrote:

I may venture to say, loosely, that in judo there is a sort of counter for every twist, wrench, pull, push or bend. Only the judo expert does not oppose such movements at all. No, he yields to them. But he does much more than yield to them. He aids them with a wicked sleight that causes the assailant to put out his own shoulder, to fracture his own arm, or in a desperate case, even to break his own neck or back.

Throws are not isolated moves; they are always performed in a fluid combat situation. As you attack, your opponent may respond with his or her own counter attack, and you must in turn respond with your combination technique. As you learn combination and counter techniques the lines will begin to blur between attack and defense. In fact, one of the paradoxes of judo is that offence is defense, defense is offence.

To succeed, your reaction to your opponent's attacks must be swift and instinctive. Your training must include practice on both the basic technique and the counters for it, so that you know them intimately. The ability to win a match or save your life in an attack comes only from diligent preparation. Many *kaeshi waza* can be used in various situations to throw your opponent, and a list of suggested techniques is provided on pages 149–151.

Attack initiative *(sen)*

Judo is a subtle and sublime art. As important as the physical aspects of judo are, it is also mentally stimulating – one reason it is considered an educational system. Students often spend considerable time and energy figuring out how to make a technique work correctly, understanding why the opponent's technique could not be avoided, and developing strategies for success.

One key strategy worth in-depth investigation involves the interplay between attack and defense. We have all heard the saying that the best defense is a good offence. In judo it is generally accepted that the key to success is to strike before your opponent has the opportunity to win. Since judo matches end when one point is achieved, there are no second chances. This teaches you to be decisive, to respond to attacks with your own attacks, and whenever possible to preempt your opponent's attacks to prevent them from being successful.

Through your practice of judo you will learn to feel your opponent's intentions the moment he or she starts to focus on an attack. It has been said that the arms are but an extension of the mind. In judo practice you are directly connected to your opponent through the arms, and it is not unusual to sense the same things as your opponent. By being aware of your opponent's grip, posture, focus, tension, movements, and so on, you can tell much about what your opponent will do next. In ice hockey they say, 'Skate to where the puck is going and not to where it has been.' In judo, the only way to get ahead of the game is to heighten your ability to perceive your opponent's intentions. To do this, your mind

Sense your opponent's intentions by feeling them with your hands.

must be relaxed and receptive, your body fluid to respond with utmost quickness to each threat. Even if you know your opponent's intentions, your conscious mind may not be able to formulate a response and direct your body to perform it in time. Both the perception of your opponent's attack and your response must be instinctive. To achieve this requires repetitive physical training, but developing a certain mental awareness is also necessary. Cultivate a mental state like a calm mountain pond, reflecting all that is around it. In Japanese this is called *mizu no kokoro* (mind like water) or *mushin* (no-mind). Your awareness can become as immediate, and your actions as instantaneous, as the moon, which is infinitely far away yet loses no time revealing its reflection on the water as soon as the clouds break.

Unlike a calm pond, judo can be a tumultuous, dynamic activity that is far from meditative. To deal with the chaos of combat, *samurai* warriors were trained to develop a combative mental state of *fudo shin* (immovable mind). This state of awareness is equated with the moon reflected in a stream: though the waters are in motion around it, the moon retains its serenity. In judo combat you move in spontaneous response to the turbulence of each situation, but your mental state should remain the same – determined and master of the self.

CHAPTER 2:
HIP THROWS
(koshi waza)

The hips (pelvis) provide the power for all hip throws. If you use them as the fulcrum of a large lever, placing them lower than your opponent's center of gravity, his upper body weight will make him tumble over you. Using your hips helps you topple opponents larger than you, using their forward momentum or weight against them.

Most, but not all, hip throws are done in a forward direction – the direction your opponent is advancing. Most techniques are described to the right side, but you must also practice the left-side version.

There are many effective ways to perform these techniques under different conditions. The techniques described in this and subsequent chapters are the most basic and standard versions, generally those taught by the Kodokan and demonstrated in promotional examinations. Some non-standard grips and applications of these techniques are shown to demonstrate alternatives. Modifications can be made for tournaments or self-defense, and we will look at some suggestions on how to do this.

Uki goshi (floating hip throw)

The favorite throw of Jigoro Kano, this is one of the simplest to apply for beginners and is in the first group of throws learned. It is also the first hip throw in the *Nage no Kata* where it is a defense against a blow to the head. While effective against an untrained opponent, it can be avoided by a knowledgeable adversary so it is seldom attempted in tournaments. It is applied to an opponent (*uke*) who is advancing forwards

KEY POINTS

• Your right arm holds *uke* around the waist and pulls his hips very tightly to your own right hip, as your left hand pulls his arm around you.

• Additional forward pull is created when you shift your weight from your right foot to your left foot, floating *uke* off his feet and onto your hip as you do so.

• By twisting your upper body to your left, *uke* will rotate around your hips. Do not bend over or lift with the legs in *uki goshi*

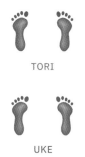

A typical foot position for the person being thrown (*uke*) is represented by the blue color. The basic foot position for the person performing the throw (*tori*) is grey. These positions can vary considerably. Note that right-side throws are shown except when the photographs demonstrate a left side throw.

TORI

UKE

To prevent your opponent from applying *uki goshi* to you, step around with your right foot to avoid hip contact, or bend the knees to lower your center of gravity. Counter with *ushiro goshi*, *utsuri goshi*, *tani otoshi*, or *sukui nage*.

If *uki goshi* does not work, follow up with another throw like *o goshi*, *harai goshi* or *kouchi gar*.

O goshi (large hip throw)

O goshi is similar to *uki goshi* except rather than twisting *uke* around your hips, your legs and hip lift *uke* up while your hands pull *uke* over your hip.

KEY POINTS
- Your right hip in *o goshi* is placed further in front of *uke* than in the previous throw.
- To apply the lifting action your feet must be between *ukes'*, with your knees bent, so your hips are under your opponent's.
- Holding *uke* tightly to your hip, pull with your hands, straighten your legs to lift *uke* off the ground, turn your upper body to your left and let *uke* fall.

If your opponent steps around your hip to escape, you can try *o goshi* again, or follow-up with *harai goshi* or *kouchi gari*. If your opponent pulls back, switch to *ouchi gari*.

You can counter an adversary who is applying *o goshi* to you with *ushiro goshi*, *utsuri goshi*, *tani otoshi*, or *sukui nage*. You may also block *o goshi*, or any forward hip or shoulder throw, with a hip smash. To accomplish this, thrust your left hip forward to meet your opponent's attacking right hip, twist your upper body and hips to your right, and sharply yank your bent right arm back. The stronger you twist and pull back with your right arm, the stronger your left hip will smash into your attacker's hip, helping you retain your balance while upsetting your attacker's.

Tsuri goshi (lifting hip throw)

KEY POINTS
- Lift *uke* strongly with the combined power of your hand lifting *uke*'s belt and your hip rising under *uke*.
- Try to get a grip on the belt before starting to attack.
- *Uke* should be off balance forward, but with a strong pull you can often defeat even a resisting opponent.

If *tsuri goshi* does not work, follow up with *harai goshi* or *ouchi gari*.

Tsuri goshi is similar to the preceding hip throws, except that you grab the belt with your hand and pull *uke* up onto your hip. There are two versions: *o tsuri goshi* (big lifting hip throw) and *ko tsuri goshi* (small lifting hip throw). In o *tsuri goshi* you reach over *uke*'s arm to grab the belt, trapping *uke*'s arm; in *ko tsuri goshi* you grab the belt after reaching under *uke*'s arm.

The foot position is generally the same as *o goshi*, but it can be done more sideways with little rotation of your hips to enter quicker and accentuate the lifting action.

VARIATION
Ko tsuri goshi

An interesting variation of *ko tsuri goshi* was taught by Mikonosuke Kawaishi, who founded the French Judo Federation. This version helps you to throw someone who squats low or is shorter than you by dropping your right leg far behind *uke*, between *uke*'s legs. This puts you under *uke* and allows you to scoop up even a defensive opponent.

Koshi guruma (hip wheel)

KEY POINTS
- Pull *uke* forward with your left hand as you slip your right hand far around *uke*'s neck.
- Bring your hip very far in front of *uke*.
- Continue rotating to your left and pull *uke* over you.

In this throw you lower your hip and roll *uke* over it like a large wheel. The center, or hub, of the wheel is your hip, while your arms and legs are the spokes. The basic position is similar to *o goshi*, but instead of placing your hand around *uke*'s waist, you place it behind the head or around the neck and use it to pull *uke* forward. Usually this hand is not gripping the jacket while throwing, so *koshi guruma* works better against an opponent whose head is up, rather than someone who is bent over and looking down. The hip position for *koshi guruma* is typically deeper than *o goshi*, and the foot position may be turned slightly more, as shown.

Tsurikomi goshi
(lifting pulling hip throw)

Tsurikomi goshi was created by Jigoro Kano in response to an opponent who stiffened up straight and pulled back to prevent *uki goshi* or *o goshi*. In *tsurikomi goshi* you drop very low so your hips make contact on *uke*'s thighs, increasing the leverage available to throw *uke*. To increase the leverage even further, maintain your right-hand grip high on *uke*'s lapel. The foot position for *tsurikomi goshi* is the same as *o goshi*. *Uke* should feel like a tall tree being toppled by the wind.

KEY POINTS
- Your right hand pulls towards the thumb like you are reeling in a big fish, while the opposite side of your hand and forearm are against the left side of *uke*'s chest.
- Do not let your right hand get behind your own head and shoulders or it will lose its strength.
- Drop as low as you can by bending the knees once you feel *uke* is off balance forwards. If *uke* is sufficiently off balance you should not feel much weight on you when you throw.

VARIATION
Taka tsurikomi goshi

In free practice, *tsurikomi goshi* may also be performed in a higher version called *taka tsurikomi goshi*, using the same hip position as *o goshi*. This allows you to use a hip throw to attack quickly without putting your arm around his waist.

Sode tsurikomi goshi
(sleeve lifting pulling hip throw)

This variation can help you to throw your opponent if you have difficulty getting low enough to apply the regular *tsurikomi goshi*. Switch your right-hand grip from *uke*'s lapel to *uke*'s left sleeve at the elbow. When you drive *uke*'s left elbow high into the air, you increase the leverage on *uke*, reducing the need to get your hips low. This throw may be used when *uke* is stiff-arming you to keep you away; since you lift strongly on the elbow you can break *uke*'s defensive grip.

KEY POINTS
- Grab *uke*'s left sleeve at the elbow with your palm up and fingers pointing to the outside.
- Push *uke*'s left elbow as high as possible to stretch your opponent out, placing your right elbow into *uke*'s armpit.
- Place your right hip in deeply as you lift and pull *uke* over you.

Harai goshi (sweeping hip throw)

KEY POINTS
- Do not attempt a sweep until *uke* is off balance, well over his right foot.
- Keep *uke*'s body tightly against yours from your lower leg all the way to your right hand by continuing a strong pull around you with your left hand.
- As your leg sweeps up, your upper thigh lifts, and your head and arms go down (along with *uke*).
- *Harai goshi* can be combined easily with *osoto gari* if your opponent changes directions. It can be blocked with the hip smash or countered with *ushiro goshi, utsuri goshi, ura nage, harai goshi gaeshi,* or *sukui nage.*

A defense for many hip throws is to step around or over your attacker's hip. *Harai goshi* is used to prevent this escape. This is the third hip throw performed in the *Nage no Kata*, but the first where you stand on one foot. It is a powerful throw often used in free practice.

Uke is generally advancing or leaning towards his or her right front when *harai goshi* is applied, but it is a versatile throw that can be used when *uke* is moving in any direction. With your left hand on the sleeve, you can maintain a normal lapel grip, grab high on the collar, or grab under the arm at the back of the shoulder blade. Pull *uke*'s right arm with determination so that *uke* puts most of his weight onto the right foot. As you enter for *harai goshi* you will continue this pull so that *uke* leans even further over the toes of the right foot.

You enter for this throw so you are supporting yourself on your left leg with your foot in front of and between *uke*'s feet. Maintaining your balance on one leg is critical since your other leg must prevent *uke* from coming around you. Using your leg in a swinging motion, you sweep *uke*'s right leg out from under him as you throw *uke* over your hip.

Hane goshi (spring hip throw)

KEY POINTS:
- The outside of your right leg contacts the inside of *uke*'s right leg.
- Point your toes down.
- Keep *uke*'s chest and abdomen tight against your side by pulling with both hands.

If *hane goshi* does not work because your opponent pulls back, your leg is in an excellent position to apply *ouchi gari* to throw *uke* to the rear, or if *uke* is off balance forward, use *uchi mata*. The primary counter attack for *hane goshi* is *hane goshi gaeshi*, but *ushiro goshi*, *utsuri goshi*, *ura nage*, or *sukui nage* (*te guruma*), may also be used.

Hane goshi was developed by Yoshitsugu Yamashita (10th dan) around 1919 when he could no longer do his favorite technique, *harai goshi*. Although knee injury prevented him from stretching his leg across his opponent's, with his leg bent he could still lift his partner into the air.

The *kuzushi* for *hane goshi* is towards *uke*'s front and slightly to the right so that *uke* is advancing onto the right foot. The entry for hane goshi is similar to *harai goshi* (opposite) except you do not turn quite as far in, maintaining more of your side in contact with *uke*'s front. Your sweeping leg is bent a little so your knee is outside of *uke*'s leg, but your foot is between *uke*'s legs. As you twist to your left, pulling *uke*, lean forward, bringing *uke* with you because of the tight contact, while your right leg raises *uke*'s right leg.

Ushiro goshi (back hip throw)

This is a reversal used against an opponent who attempts a hip or shoulder throw on you. When *uke* enters for a throw like *o goshi*, bend your knees to drop your hips lower than *uke* and pull *uke* tightly against your chest and stomach. Lift *uke* by straightening your legs as you thrust your hips forward and lean backwards. *uke* should feel like a large wave has come in from behind, sweeping out *uke*'s legs and floating *uke* onto the crest of the wave. Throw *uke* by stepping backwards with your left foot and dropping *uke* in front of you.

KEY POINTS
- Spoil your opponent's attack first by sinking low; then perform the counter-throw.
- Hold *uke* tightly against your body.
- Lift *uke* as high as possible using strong hip action.

When *ushiro goshi* does not work, follow it up with *utsuri goshi* or *ura nage*. If someone is attempting this throw on you, counter with an effective *sukui nage* or *kosoto gari*.

Utsuri goshi (hip shift)

This throw begins with the same lifting action as *ushiro goshi* (opposite), but the throwing action is different. Instead of stepping back to finish the throw, step forward so *uke* will fall onto your hip and you can finish with a hip throw like *o goshi*. Sometimes *harai goshi* is used to finish the throw instead. *Utsuri goshi* is particularly useful when the *ushiro goshi* is weak, and *uke*'s legs continue to hang down in such a way that they would land on the mat, making it difficult for you to throw *uke* onto his back. In *utsuri goshi*, *uke* is lifted into the air face up, then flipped completely over in one complete turn to land on the mat face up again.

KEY POINTS
- Hold *uke* tightly to your body with your arms.
- Bend your knees to get under *uke* so you can arch your back and use the power of your hips to lift *uke* high on your chest.
- Before *uke*'s feet come down on the ground, move your hip into position for the final hip throw

CHAPTER 3:
HAND THROWS
(te waza)

All throws involve nearly every part of the body acting in a coordinated manner. Hand throws are no exception, although the emphasis here is the action of the hands, arms and shoulders. In some cases only the hands make contact with the opponent, while in other cases your hip or leg will help the throw by blocking *uke*.

The beauty of hand throws is that you can react quickly to take advantage of any weakness in *uke's* balance while still transferring the power of your entire body into the throw. Your hands should always be in contact with your opponent, providing the means to upset his balance in very subtle—or quite dramatic—ways. Your arms may simply pull to encourage *uke* to move, or push to shift *uke's* weight. In other throws, you may use your arms to turn, lift, trip or roll *uke*. For success in *te waza*, focus on the effective use of your hands, arms and shoulders without neglecting proper body mechanics or your opponent's movement.

Seoi nage (shoulder throw)

Seoi nage is one of the most successful throws seen in tournaments of all levels. It was a favorite technique of Japanese superstar Ryoko Tani (Tamura), who used it successfully while dominating the extra lightweight (-48kg) weight class to win seven World Championship titles and two Olympic gold medals. She retired from competition in 2010 after almost 20 years where she was only defeated 5 times. The International Judo Federation named her "best female judoka ever."

Seoi nage can be applied in a number of ways and has many variations. The basic idea is to start with a normal grip, turn so that *uke* is pulled onto your back with your knees bent deeply, then drive forward and throw *uke* over your shoulder to the ground. Apply this technique when *uke* is moving, pushing or leaning forward.

Many other specialized versions of *seoi nage* use variations of the basic hand or foot position. In a version called *eri seoi nage*, the right hand grabs *uke*'s right lapel instead of the left. Other versions include reverse *seoi nage* where you rotate strongly and throw *uke* more to the side or backwards, *ganseki otoshi* with a grip on both lapels, and *hantaigawa no seoi nage*, or inside-out shoulder throw, applied to *uke*'s opposite arm entering from the outside (*uke*'s left arm is over your right shoulder).

Seoi nage may also use different foot positions. Sometimes your right leg is used to block *uke*'s advancing right foot, similar to the foot position for *tai otoshi*. Alternatively, you can place your straightened right leg deep between *uke*'s legs. You may even drop to your knees to perform *seoi nage*, then lift and drive forward. In each case, what defines *seoi nage* is that it is a lifting throw where *uke* is picked up onto your back.

Seoi nage is combined effectively with backward throws since that is the direction *uke* will generally resist. *Ouchi gari* and *kouchi gari* are excellent preparatory or follow-up attacks. This throw may be countered with *ushiro goshi*, or *ura nage*.

KEY POINTS

- Turn the right hand into the lapel so it is not bent backwards.
- Bend your knees to get as low as possible.
- As you throw, rotate your shoulders to the left, pulling *uke* over you. Turn your head to the left and bring your hands toward your left knee as you rotate.

Hantai gawa no seoi nage

Drop-knee seoi nage

Ippon seoi nage
(one-arm shoulder throw)

This version of *seoi nage* is performed in *Nage no Kata* (forms of throwing) in response to an overheard blow. A popular tournament technique, is it also important for self-defense since it can be done without a *judogi* in response to a variety of attacks, and can be used to break the arm if necessary.

KEY POINTS

- Start the *kuzushi* with a good pull from your left hand upward and forward, then enter and place *uke*'s arm well below the point of your own shoulder. Place your right arm tight into *uke*'s armpit so the back of your shoulder and upper back are in close contact with *uke*'s front.
- Bend your legs to get as low as possible so you can hoist *uke* onto your back.
- As you throw, pull both hands down and to your left to pull *uke* over you. Turn your head to the left and bring your hands towards your left knee as you rotate your upper body.

One unorthodox way of performing *ippon seoi nage* is to apply the right-sided throw attacking *uke*'s left arm. It may also be performed against both of *uke*'s arms by gripping both sleeves.

If you miss the throw and go completely under *uke*'s arm, turn in for a *morote gari*. If *uke* resists backwards, attack with *osoto gari* or *kouchi gari*.

Ippon seoi nage may be countered with *tani otoshi*, *ushiro goshi* or *ura nage*.

VARIATION
Self-defense version with arm bar

VARIATION
Two-handed variation

VARIATION
Inside-out

Kata guruma (shoulder wheel)

Jigoro Kano learned this technique while studying *Tenshin Shinyo Ryu Jujutsu* as a young man. One of the advanced students was Fukushima, a large man Kano could not throw no matter how hard he tried, so he researched other methods to gain an advantage. He adapted a throw from wrestling to devise *kata guruma*, eventually using it to throw the mighty Fukushima. It is now included in the *Nage no Kata*.

KEY POINTS

- For maximum leverage and balance try to place *uke*'s waist directly behind your neck.
- Sink low and rise up as *uke*'s weight falls onto your shoulders. Keep your back straight up and use your legs to lift.
- Continue pulling with your left hand throughout the throw.

The traditional way to perform *kata guruma* is to pull *uke* continuously forward with your left hand while you drop under *uke* and grab *uke*'s right leg with your right arm. *Uke* should be pulled onto your shoulders so you can stand up and throw *uke* down. The throw can also be performed on one or both knees between *uke*'s legs. In competition it is also seen in a version that is more like a sacrifice throw: your left leg slides onto the mat in front of *uke*'s right foot and your left hip comes to the ground under *uke*. *Uke* is thrown to his right front corner as you fall onto the left side.

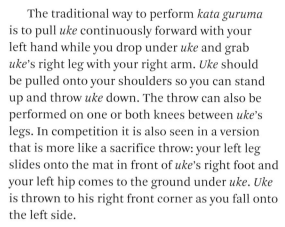

VARIATION
Kata guruma on one knee

Kata guruma as a sacrifice throw

In competition it is also seen in a version that is more like a sacrifice throw: your left leg slides onto the mat in front of *uke*'s right foot and your left hip comes to the ground under *uke*. *Uke* is thrown to his right front corner as you fall onto the left side.

Tai otoshi (body drop)

In this throw you pull *uke* off balance as *uke* is stepping forward with the right foot. Your right leg blocks *uke*'s advancing foot and *uke*'s upper body is pulled forward, then rotated down to the ground. *Tai otoshi* may sometimes be done more towards the right side if *uke* is moving in that direction. Because it is performed entirely with the hands, but without hip contact, using *uke*'s momentum is essential.

KEY POINTS
- Spread your legs far apart for a stable base, with slightly more of your weight on your left leg.
- Block *uke*'s right leg below the knee with your right calf so *uke*'s weight can come forward over his foot. Your right leg should be bent slightly before you apply the throw.
- Pull around you with your left hand and push with your right hand to rotate *uke*'s body, then twist your upper body and turn your head to the left.

Tai otoshi is often used in combination with *uchi mata* or *ouchi gari*. If *uke* escapes your *tai otoshi* attempt by stepping over your leg, apply *tai otoshi* again since he is already moving in the direction you want to throw. One way to counter it is to step your right foot over the attacking leg and apply *kouchi gari* with your left foot.

Sukui nage (scooping throw)

- Bend your right leg at almost a 90-degree angle so *uke* can fall over it.
- Grab both legs securely with your hands and hang on until *uke* is on the floor.
- Push *uke* backwards with your hips and shoulder as you scoop the legs.

This is usually applied as a counter to a hip throw, or when your opponent has one foot well in front of the other. After you get behind *uke*, scoop out *uke*'s legs and throw *uke* over your leg directly onto his back. Sometimes to add power or control *uke's* landing, or if the *uke* hangs on to you, you will fall backwards onto *uke*. In a self-defense situation it may be used to counter a headlock or rear naked choke.

Te guruma (hand wheel)

A variation of *sukui nage,* often called *te guruma,* was used by Robert van de Walle to win the gold medal match at the 1980 Olympics. *Uke* is scooped off the mats using your hands aided by the forward thrust of your hips. As a counter throw, it is an ever-present threat to *osoto gari, harai goshi* and *uchi mata*, demonstrating the significant power that can be generated if you anticipate an attack and harmonize with *uke*'s movement.

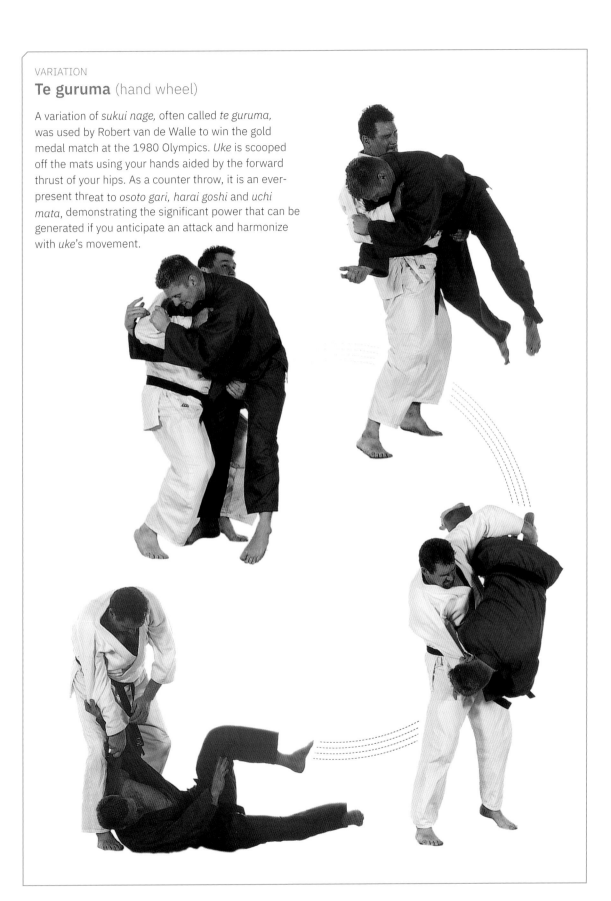

Obi otoshi (belt drop)

This is similar to *sukui nage* in the foot position and the direction you throw your opponent (backward). However, the hand position is different and you can sometimes achieve a better lifting action. Grab the front of *uke*'s belt with your left hand, palm up, then reach across *uke*'s body with your right hand to grab the opposite arm, hip, or upper thigh.

KEY POINTS
- Pull strongly with the hand on the belt to force *uke* to lean backwards to regain balance.
- Take advantage of the opportunity by entering quickly.
- Straighten your legs and push your hips forward as you lift *uke*.

Sumi otoshi (corner drop)

This is similar to *uki otoshi* as both are sometimes called air throws; here, however, the angle of attack is to *uke*'s right rear instead of forward. This throw is usually performed when *uke* is stepping forward, but can be applied as he is turning, moving to his right side, or beginning to move back as long as *uke*'s weight is on the right heel. Advance strongly with your left foot, as you would for *osoto gari*, and rotate *uke* with a motion similar to a hard left turn on a steering wheel.

KEY POINTS
- Use this throw when *uke* is advancing and you have a chance to rapidly reverse *uke*'s motion in a circular fashion.
- Pull out and then down sharply with your left hand on *uke*'s sleeve as you step forward with your left foot.
- Use your right hand first to pull *uke* close and break his balance to the right rear, then, with the power of your forward momentum, to push *uke*'s right shoulder up and over the left arm.

Uki otoshi (floating drop)

The first throw in the *Nage no Kata*, this is the classic demonstration of a hand throw since no other part of your body comes in contact with *uke*. It can be performed either on one knee, as it is in the *Nage no Kata*, or from a standing position, as it is more commonly used in competition.

KEY POINTS

- Use this throw when *uke* is advancing strongly and you have the opportunity to quickly extend *uke*'s center of gravity beyond his feet utilizing *uke*'s forward momentum.
- Continue to pull *uke* forward, then pull down sharply with your left hand on the sleeve as you step back with your left foot and drop down onto your left knee.
- Pull *uke* past you with your right hand, then rotate *uke* down to the mat.

VARIATION
Uki otoshi standing

Seoi otoshi (shoulder drop)

Shown here as a self-defense response to a rear choke, *seoi otoshi* is similar to *seoi nage* except that *uke* is not lifted up, but dropped straight down. *Otoshi* means to let fall, so you must get low under *uke*. It relies on your dropping action to generate power. *Tori* drops to one knee between *uke*'s legs (see foot diagram), outside *uke*'s legs (see the photographs), or puts both knees on the mat between *uke*'s legs.

KEY POINTS
- Pull *uke* forward or take advantage of *uke*'s forward push.
- As you drop down under *uke,* utilize your body weight to pull him with you and over your shoulder.
- Be careful to protect *uke*'s head from hitting the ground.

Obi tori gaeshi (belt grab reversal)

This throw was popularized by Shota Khabareli who earned a gold medal in the 1980 Olympics representing the Soviet Union. Until recognized by the Kodokan in 2017 as *obi tori gaeshi* it was often called the Khabareli.

When your opponent is bent over, reach over his right shoulder and grab the belt with your right hand. With your left hand grab his pants near his right knee or lower thigh. Step in deeply between *uke*'s legs, apply the front of your right thigh inside *uke*'s left thigh. Combining the lift from your hands and your right leg, arch your back, thrust your hips forward, and lift *uke* up and over to his left front in a rolling motion. This may also be done without assistance from the leg, and your left hand may grab the belt instead of the leg.

KEY POINTS
- When your opponent is resisting by bending over, take advantage of the opportunity by reaching over *uke*'s right shoulder to grab the belt keeping him bent over.
- Immediately grab *uke*'s pants with your left hand then lift with the help of your right knee boosting *uke* up.
- Keep *uke*'s head down with your right arm to help roll him over.

Yama arashi (mountain storm)

- Grip securely with both hands on *uke*'s right sleeve and right lapel.
- Rotate *uke* around you with the pull of both hands.
- Block *uke* from advancing with your right leg.

VARIATION
Self-defense version

Shiro Saigo, one of the four Heavenly Lords of early judo, made this throw famous, using it to win against early *jujutsu* masters in a tournament that led to the adoption of judo training by the Tokyo Metropolitan Police. It uses a whipping action, rotating *uke* around your base like the tempestuous winds of a mountain storm. Grab the top of *uke*'s right sleeve with both hands (see self-defense variation), or grab *uke*'s right lapel with your right hand, thumb inside. Place your right foot across *uke*'s right leg, below the knee.

Morote gari (two-hand reap)

In wrestling, this throw is called a double-leg takedown. *Uke*'s legs are grabbed and pulled out as *uke* falls backwards. You can use a powerful forward drive, a sharp lifting action, or both. You can reap *uke*'s legs out to the front or to the side.

KEY POINTS
- Your hands should grab around *uke*'s legs as far and as tightly as possible.
- Push with your shoulder into *uke*'s body, and keep your head up.
- Lift and reap the legs by strongly pulling them out from under *uke* in the opposite direction from where you are pushing.

VARIATION
Lifting, sweeping legs to the side

Kibisu gaeshi (heel trip)

Deceptively simple, but very effective, this technique is generally applied to *uke*'s forward leg when *uke* is advancing. The attack may be applied with either hand grabbing the right ankle. It may also be applied from the outside using the right hand to grab the right foot. *Uke* may continue his forward progress or, if he is retreating, fall backwards.

KEY POINTS
- As *uke* steps forward with the right foot, pull *uke*'s weight to your left.
- Drop down quickly and grab *uke*'s heel or ankle.
- Continue the pull to *uke*'s right front as you lift the heel.

COMBINATION
Throwing with kibisu gaeshi after your opponent evades your seoi otoshi attack

Kouchi gaeshi
(small inner-reaping throw)

This is a counter throw used against an opponent who tries *kouchi gari*. As *uke* enters for *kouchi gari* against your right foot, lift your foot to escape the attack, step back to further unbalance *uke*, and twist to your left, throwing *uke* in front of you. If *uke* pushes more to your right, you can place your right foot on *uke*'s left knee, twist to your right, and apply *hiza guruma*.

- Maintain your balance while escaping the attack and turn sharply.
- Take control of *uke*'s balance while he enters on one foot by pulling him in the direction you will turn.
- Rotate *uke*'s upper body as you twist and pull him around you.

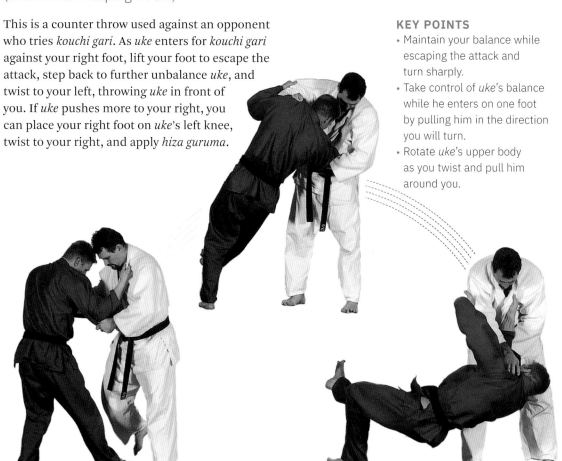

VARIATION
Hiza guruma version

Kuchiki taoshi
(one-hand or dead-tree drop)

KEY POINTS
- Use this technique when *uke* is straight, not bent over.
- Grab *uke*'s leg with as much of your arm as possible, and lift it high quickly.
- Drive straight back as you enter, but after lifting *uke*'s leg turn somewhat to your left.

Step deeply between *uke*'s legs with your right foot, reaching down with your left hand to grab *uke*'s right leg. Lift the leg as you drive *uke* backward with your body and right hand. This throw can be applied as a counter to *hiza guruma*, or in combination with *kouchi gari* or *ouchi gari*.

Uchi mata sukashi
(inner-thigh throw reversal)

KEY POINTS
- When your opponent attacks with a left side *uchi mata*, bring your right knee close to your left knee as quickly as possible so *uke*'s attacking leg cannot get between your legs.
- Pull with your left hand gripping the sleeve and push with your right hand as you roll *uke* forward in the direction of his attack.
- Bring your body close to increase power.

This is a popular counter to a fast *uchi mata*. To perform it you must sense the oncoming attack, slide your leg out of the way so that *uke* misses it, then use your hands to throw *uke* forward in a rolling motion.

CHAPTER 4:
LEG THROWS
(ashi waza)

Ashi waza are throws that rely primarily on attacking an opponent's lower body with your legs or feet. In some you move *uke's* feet out from under him; in others you stop his feet from moving when his upper body continues in motion. *Ashi waza* tend to be fast attacks that rely on catching your opponent at a weak moment, so accurate timing is the most critical element.

Because strength is less of a factor, *ashi waza* are often effective against larger opponents. Many are used in combination with other throws. Skill in *ashi waza* helps make other throws possible and allows you to attack from a greater distance than other types of techniques. They
are equally important for breaking down a strong defense and against someone trying to advance on you.

In leg throws you generally reap, sweep, hook, or block your opponent's leg or legs. Reaping (*gari*) throws involve cutting out *uke's* leg as if you are swinging a scythe; sweeping (*harai*) throws involve more subtle timing so *uke's* foot is moved as his weight shifts towards it. Hooking (*gake*) throws trap *uke's* weight-bearing foot in place as you push *uke* over it. Blocking (*sasae*) and wheeling (*guruma*) throws use your leg to stop *uke* from advancing or retreating while your hands drive *uke* over.

Deashi harai
(forward or advancing foot sweep)

This is one of the simplest throws to learn, but applying it in practice is quite difficult. Since timing is crucial, practice it repeatedly in *randori*. Used against an opponent untrained in judo it can be both easy and devastating.

Uke will be stepping forward, shifting weight from the back foot to the front foot. To do so, *uke* must lean slightly forward and have some forward momentum. Once the forward motion starts, *uke* is committed to stepping and cannot go back without putting the front foot on the ground. Your task is to continue *uke*'s forward motion while sweeping *uke*'s foot out before too much weight is placed on it. Avoid sweeping too early before *uke* has committed to the step, or too late after weight is placed on the foot and it cannot be moved. Do not give away your intentions by any strong hand action until after you have swept the foot. Invite *uke* to come willingly towards you.

Deashi harai is a popular throw to set up an opponent for *tai otoshi* or *harai goshi*. It can be applied from quite a distance, and with only a one-handed grip on *uke*'s sleeve. To escape the throw *uke* must either put weight on the front foot so it cannot be swept, or put weight on the back foot and lift the front foot out of the sweep. *Uke* can then counterattack with *tsubame gaeshi*.

KEY POINTS
- Try to sweep with the sole of your foot, placing the ball of your foot around *uke*'s heel, and keep your sweeping leg almost straight so you feel the power of your hips in the sweep.
- Sweep *uke*'s foot forward in the direction it is moving, or somewhat across *uke*'s body.
- Pull your left hand down following your left leg, and push your right hand toward your left. Use your hands as if you are turning the steering wheel on a large truck.

Hiza guruma (knee wheel)

This was a favorite throw of Dutchman Anton Geesink, who was awarded the rank of 10th dan by the IJF, and was the first non-Japanese judo competitor to win the World Championships (1961) and Olympic gold (1964).

It takes advantage of *uke*'s forward motion to throw. As *uke* advances, add your own power to help *uke* advance even faster, then stop *uke* from stepping forward while continuing the momentum of the upper body in a circular motion.

KEY POINTS:
- Step quickly to the right and turn towards your left while pulling *uke* around you with your left hand.
- Place the sole of your left foot on the bottom side of *uke*'s right kneecap to prevent *uke* from stepping.
- Keep your left leg almost straight and continue your turn to the left to throw *uke* over your left leg.

This throw is often combined with *osoto gari* and countered by grabbing the attacking leg and trying *kuchiki taoshi* or *ouchi gari*.

Sasae tsurikomi ashi
(propping lifting pulling throw)

This throw is embodied in the *samurai* saying, 'When the enemy comes welcome him; when he goes send him on his way.' First invite *uke* in close, then block the advancing ankle with speed and accuracy as you move out of the way so *uke* flies past. Fearlessly draw *uke* into you and then twist with sudden determination to bring *uke* around you and to the ground.

KEY POINTS:
- Bring the sole of your left foot strongly against the front of *uke*'s advancing right ankle.
- Keep *uke* close to you, bringing your own right hip near *uke*'s left hip.
- Rotate your body strongly to your left bringing *uke* around with you.

Osoto gari (large outer reap)

This powerful throw, frequently used in self-defense and tournaments, is a favorite of Yasuhiro Yamashita, who won four World Championships leading up to his Olympic gold medal in 1984.

To perform this throw, push with your hands and body to *uke*'s right rear corner, then continue relentlessly to drive into *uke* as you sweep out the supporting leg, causing *uke* to fall backwards. Keep your toes pointed and your leg strong, making your body one long lever as you reap.

KEY POINTS

- As you drive forward, pin *uke* across your chest with your left hand.
- Bring your right leg and hip through very far for a powerful sweep.
- As you sweep, bring your head down and your foot up at least as high as your head, and at the same time twist to your left.

Osoto gari can be combined with *harai goshi* or *hiza guruma*. The basic counter is *osoto gaeshi*. *Harai goshi* may also be used.

Osoto gaeshi
(large outer reap counter)

In this counter your opponent is attacking your right leg with *osoto gari*. Block the attack early by quickly stepping forward with your left foot and driving *uke* back (as shown). Apply your own *osoto gari*. If *tori* has already broken your balance backwards, step back with your left foot to regain your balance while twisting and pulling *uke* to your left before striking with your own *osoto gari*.

KEY POINTS
- When you step with your left foot, pull your left hand strongly to bring *uke* with you.
- Rotate your body strongly to your left, and push *uke*'s head to your left as you turn.
- Once *uke* is off balance, reap out the leg.

Osoto otoshi (large outer drop)

This is similar to *osoto gari*, but in the final throwing action you do not reap *uke*'s leg out. Cut *uke* down by slicing your leg into the back of *uke*'s leg to drive his hip forward, bend his knee, break his posture backwards, and drop him to the mat.

KEY POINTS
- Raise your attacking leg high, with a bent knee.
- Try to place the back of your foot or calf at the top of *uke*'s thigh, then drive it down between *uke*'s legs as you straighten it.
- Push *uke* straight down onto his back.

Osoto guruma (large outer wheel)

This is similar to *osoto gari*, but both *uke*'s legs are blocked while *uke* is thrown directly backward. *Uke*'s legs must be relatively close together for it to work. Use it as a counter or follow-up to *osoto gari* and *kosoto gari*. To defeat it, use *osoto gaeshi*.

KEY POINTS

- Both hands force *uke* back and then down to the rear.
- Step in very deep and keep your body close to *uke*. Your right hip must penetrate past *uke*'s hip.
- Place your right leg across *uke*'s legs, your right ankle behind *uke*'s left knee. Drive back and down to wheel *uke* over your leg

Ouchi gari (large inner reap)

This technique was often used by the 1987 World Champion, Mike Swain, of the United States. Perform the basic throw while *uke* is advancing with the left leg, reaping it out as it moves forward, causing *uke* to fall. There are many possible variations, set-ups and follow-ups.

KEY POINTS

- As *uke* steps forward, pull *uke* more forward with your right hand so the right side of your chest comes in contact with *uke*'s chest.
- Place your right leg behind *uke*'s left leg and reap it in the direction it is moving.
- *Uke* should fall backward toward the leg being reaped.

This technique is often used in combination with *uchi mata* or *kouchi gari* since your leg is already between *uke*'s. To counter it use *ouchi gaeshi* (opposite) or *tani otoshi*.

Ouchi gaeshi
(large inner reap counter)

When you are attacked with *ouchi gari* against your left leg, sweep *uke*'s leg across your body and throw *uke* to your left. A variation of this throw is to rotate *uke* to the right as you escape the reap, throwing with a motion such as *uki otoshi*.

KEY POINTS
- Control *uke*'s head as the attack begins.
- Rotate your upper body to the left, bringing *uke* with you.
- Use your entire leg to sweep *uke*'s leg to your right.

VARIATION

Kosoto gake (small outer hook)

This is similar to *kosoto gari* except that you do not reap *uke*'s foot out. Instead, you hold it in place so it cannot move and you push *uke* over it.

KEY POINTS
- Hook your heel around the back of *uke*'s heel.
- Pull down and to your left with your left hand, while pushing *uke* back and to your left with your right hand.
- Try to pin all of *uke*'s weight onto the outside edge of *uke*'s right heel.

This throw may also be done in a very low version where you wrap your leg around *uke*'s ankle so that your knee is behind *uke*'s heel. You may be able to follow this throw with *osoto gari* if *uke* escapes. *Uchi mata* is the most common counter throw.

Kouchi gari (small inner reap)

This is an especially effective throw against an opponent whose legs are spread too far apart. Whenever your opponent's feet are more than shoulder width apart, you should be able to reap one foot out with this throw.

Kouchi gari is often combined with *ouchi gari* or *uchi mata* into an integrated attack. It can be countered with a well-timed *hiza guruma* or *kouchi gaeshi*.

Kosoto gari (small outer reap)

This small reap is applied to *uke*'s foot, rather than the entire leg as in osoto gari, which is a big reaping action. As there is less power in a smaller reaping movement you need better timing and less weight on the foot you are attacking. This throw is usually used while *uke* is moving forward onto the foot you want to attack.

Nidan kosoto gari is a variation usually applied when you attack with *kosoto gari* but *uke* lifts his foot in the air, so you quickly reap out the other foot while you continue pushing *uke* backwards. You can counter a weak *kosoto gari* attack with *osoto gari*, or a more powerful attack by turning into *uchi mata*.

KEY POINTS
- Use this throw when *uke* is stepping forward.
- Use the sole of your foot behind *uke*'s heel to reap it forward in the direction that *uke*'s toes are pointing.
- Pull *uke* to your left with your left hand while your body and right arm push *uke* backward.

Uchi mata (inner-thigh throw)

This is one of the most powerful and popular throws in competitive judo. Although classified as a leg throw in the *Nage no Kata*, it can also be applied with a significant amount of hip action.

KEY POINTS:
- Pull *uke* forward to create the *kuzushi*, or apply the technique when *uke* is off balance to the front.
- With your upper thigh, try to lift *uke*'s right thigh, but you may attack anywhere between *uke*'s left thigh and right thigh.
- As your leg sweeps up, bring your upper body down twisting to your left, bringing *uke* with you.

Use *uchi mata* after trying attacks with *ouchi gari* or *kouchi gari*. The primary counter is *uchi mata sukashi*.

Ashi guruma (leg wheel)

Pull *uke* forward, then quickly block the advancing leg and pull *uke* over it. This throw is similar in principle to *hiza guruma*, but with the difference that you are facing the opposite direction and applying the technique with the opposite foot.

KEY POINTS:
- Place your right leg across *uke*'s right leg around the knee.
- Continue a strong pull around you and down with your left hand while pushing with your right.
- Throw *uke* straight forward, although you can also throw more towards the side.

Harai tsurikomi ashi
(lifting pulling foot sweep)

KEY POINTS:
- As *uke*'s left foot steps back, enter close and place the sole of your right foot on the front of *uke*'s left ankle.
- Keeping your right leg straight, sweep *uke*'s left foot back and to your left.
- Simultaneously pull *uke*'s upper body around you to your right.

This looks somewhat like *sasae tsurikomi ashi*. However, it is applied when *uke* is retreating rather than advancing, and *uke*'s legs are swept out rather than simply blocked.

O guruma (large wheel)

This is a forward throw similar in appearance to *harai goshi*. The difference is that your leg contacts *uke* higher and you are further away from *uke* so your leg cannot sweep and only blocks while you wheel *uke*'s chest over it. This was a specialty of Kyuzo Mifune, the fourth of only 15 10th degree black belts ever promoted by the Kodokan. He found it an easy way for a small person to throw a larger person.

KEY POINTS
- As *uke* is coming forward, use the spinning entry shown below, and place your thigh just below *uke*'s waist.
- Continue bringing *uke*'s upper body forward with your hands and your turning motion.
- Use your leg like a bar to roll *uke* over.

Okuriashi harai
(following foot sweep)

As *uke* moves sideways or in a circular motion, the feet generally slide apart and then together. This throw takes advantage of this natural motion by sliding *uke*'s feet further to the side so they slip out from under *uke* as if they are on ice. Always sweep *uke*'s feet in the direction they are moving to accelerate their motion, while stopping *uke*'s upper body from following. Use this throw when *uke* is stepping around you or directly to the side. The faster *uke* is moving, the better the throw will work, but your timing must be impeccable.

KEY POINTS
- Use the sole of your foot on the outside of *uke*'s ankle to sweep it sideways towards *uke*'s other foot.
- Keep your sweeping leg relatively straight in line with your torso so you use the power of your entire body as one long, coordinated lever.
- Lift and turn *uke*'s upper body with your hands.

When your foot's sweeping action misses, follow up with *tai otoshi* or *harai goshi*. This throw can be countered with *tsubame gaeshi*, or you can step through and apply *tai otoshi* or *harai goshi*.

Tsubame gaeshi (swallow counter)

When your opponent tries *deashi harai* against you, lift your foot off the mat and quickly sweep the attacking foot with your own *deashi harai*. Your foot will make a quick circular motion like the flight of a swallow.

KEY POINTS

- Try to move your foot out of the way just before *uke* makes contact with your foot.
- Bend your knee without moving your upper leg so your foot comes back quickly; then straighten your knee again to place your foot against *uke*'s foot.
- Take control of the throw with your hands.

Uchi mata gaeshi
(inner thigh throw counter),

Harai goshi gaeshi
(sweeping hip throw counter),

Hane goshi gaeshi
(spring hip throw counter)

These three techniques differ mainly in the attacks that are offered by *uke*. In each case you counter *uke*'s attempted throw – *uchi mata*, *harai goshi* or *hane goshi* – by throwing *uke* to the side or back corner. *Uchi mata gaeshi* is shown below.

KEY POINTS
- Pull your right hand back and step to your left as *uke* enters for the throw, bringing *uke* off balance to the left.
- Place your left foot around *uke*'s supporting leg.
- Continue moving *uke* to the left, blocking or sweeping out *uke*'s supporting leg with your left foot or leg.

CHAPTER 5:
SACRIFICE THROWS
(sutemi waza)

Any technique in which you must give up your standing position and fall to the ground to throw your opponent is called a sacrifice throw. Sacrifice means you intentionally put yourself in danger in order to gain a greater objective.

Sacrifice throws are risky in free practice and tournaments; if your attempt is unsuccessful your opponent will usually be in a superior position over you. Even so, sacrifice techniques are often attempted in international competition, and can be extremely effective because they utilize gravity more than strength to build momentum. *Sutemi waza* skills allow you to get as low as possible under your opponent, while using your entire body weight to add power.

There are traditionally two types of sacrifice throws: those where you fall to your side (*yoko sutemi waza*); and those where you fall to your back (*ma sutemi waza*). The lines between these groups are often blurred since some throws can be done either way.

Tomoe nage (circular throw)

Use *tomoe nage* when *uke* is advancing strongly or leaning forward. It also works well against an opponent who is using stiff arms to prevent you from getting close. As *uke* pushes, you suddenly give way, like a dam breaking, so *uke* crashes forward and tumbles down. This throw is seen quite often in tournaments, as well as various films.

Other variations of this throw include a two-foot version, and *yoko tomoe nage*, where you fall to your side under *uke* to throw sideways. Foot sweeps often lead into *tomoe nage* attacks. A well-timed *ouchi gari* or *kouchi gari* may work as a counter if you successfully anticipate the attack, or enter immediately into *newaza* while blocking or sliding off the attacking foot.

VARIATION
Yoko tomoe nage

Sumi gaeshi (corner reversal)

This is typically used against an opponent in a bent-over, defensive posture. It is similar to *tomoe nage* except the foot position is not as high on *uke*, which makes it easier to do against an opponent who is in a very low posture, or who is very close to you. *Sumi gaeshi* is very similar to sweeps used to roll over an opponent once you are on your back on the ground, so learning it will help in other grappling situations as well.

KEY POINTS
- Pull *uke* forward and down, controlling *uke*'s right arm.
- As you fall to your back under *uke* place the top of your right foot on the inside of *uke*'s left thigh.
- Use your foot to lift *uke* as your hands pull *uke* forward (*uke* typically rolls over his right shoulder).

Tani otoshi (valley drop)

Tani otoshi is often used as a counter attack to a hip or shoulder throw, but can also be applied when *uke* pulls back to recover from your attempted hip throw. *Uke* should feel as if his feet are on the edge of a cliff and he is falling backward into a deep valley.

KEY POINTS
- Drive your right leg behind both of *uke*'s legs.
- Keep *uke*'s side tight against your chest.
- Turn towards *uke* so that you land on top as you fall to your right.

Uki waza (floating technique)

KEY POINTS
- Slide your left leg very deep in front of *uke's* advancing right foot so your upper thigh blocks *uke's* advance.
- Use your falling weight to bring *uke's* upper body forward and down.
- Turn to your left side as you throw *uke* over your left shoulder.

Uki waza is performed lightly with little physical contact, so when *uke* comes at you he rolls like a tumbleweed blown through a deserted town.

Yoko otoshi (side drop)

This is similar to *uki waza* (above) except for the direction of the throw. As you drop to your side, throw *uke* directly sideways over your outstretched leg, not forward as in *uki waza*.

KEY POINTS
- Slide your left leg in very far so your upper thigh comes close to the outside of *uke's* right foot.
- Use your falling weight to pull *uke* off balance to the side.
- Turn your body towards your left side as you throw.

Yoko wakare (side separation)

For this throw, roll *uke* over and around your upper body as you fall directly on your side in front of *uke*. Your falling action brings *uke* forward and down, while rotating your body rolls *uke* over you.

KEY POINTS
- Fall directly in front of *uke* as *uke* is pushing forward and advancing.
- Pull *uke*'s upper body tightly to you as you fall so that *uke* is sure to come down with you.
- As you fall, twist strongly to your left bringing *uke* over you.

Yoko guruma (side wheel)

This is commonly used as a counter to an opponent's strong forward hip or shoulder throw. Go with the attacker's throwing action, even accelerating it, falling in front of *uke* and pulling him over you to complete the throw. *Uke*'s own drive forward causes him to fall over you. This is seldom used in tournaments because in a good *yoko guruma* there is no break between your opponent's attack and your application of *yoko guruma*, so the referee often gives the score to your opponent when you fall onto your back, not considering that he was subsequently thrown.

KEY POINTS
- As *uke* attempts a hip throw such as *uki goshi*, slide around the attacking hip, swinging your right leg deep between *uke*'s legs.
- Place your left hand around *uke*'s waist and the palm of your right hand on *uke*'s stomach.
- Fall close under *uke*, deep between *uke*'s legs, and roll *uke* over your left shoulder.

Ura nage (back throw)

When *uke* attacks for a hip or shoulder throw with insufficient forward drive, drop low to pick *uke* up and throw him over your shoulder as you fall to your back. Commonly called a suplex in wrestling, this throw can be done easily without any grip on the *judogi*. *Uke* can stop or counter this throw by hooking a leg and reversing direction, as in *ouchi gari*.

KEY POINTS
- As *uke* comes close for a hip or shoulder throw, bend your legs to get low under *uke*.
- Grab tightly around *uke*'s waist with both hands to hold *uke*'s body against your chest.
- Lift *uke* by straightening your legs and thrusting your hips forward, then fall to your back, throwing *uke* over your left shoulder.

Hikikomi gaeshi
(pulling-in counter)

KEY POINTS
- Using your left hand for leverage, push *uke*'s right shoulder up. When *uke* resists, reverse direction and pull the shoulder down as you fall under *uke*.
- Rotate to your right as you slide under *uke*.
- Pull *uke*'s belt to bring *uke* over you to his left front corner.

This throw is used against an opponent in a bent-over, defensive position. It can also be used when your opponent is on hands and knees in front of you. Pull *uke*'s head down so you can put your chest on it. With your left arm grab under *uke*'s right arm and place your hand on *uke*'s right shoulder blade. Grab the back of *uke*'s belt with your right hand to pull *uke* over you as you fall under him.

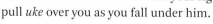

Yoko gake (side hook)

In *yoko gake*, off-balance *uke* to the outside edge of his advanced foot, then hook it with your foot. Falling down on your side, use your momentum to thrust your foot in a sweeping action. *Uke* falls next to you like a tall tree after it is chopped off at the bottom. This technique is usually studied in depth when learning the *Nage no Kata*.

KEY POINTS
- Straighten *uke* upright as you pull *uke*'s right sleeve into your chest, bringing his weight onto his advanced right foot.
- Place your left foot strongly against the side of *uke*'s foot.
- Fall to your left side as you cut *uke*'s feet out, bringing *uke* down next to you.

Tawara gaeshi (rice bale counter)

This is typically used as a counter to *morote gari* or any double-leg takedown or tackle. It can also be performed against an opponent in a bent-over, defensive posture.

KEY POINTS
- As *uke* grabs around your waist or legs, reach over *uke*'s back and around *uke*'s waist with both hands.
- Grab your own wrist in front of *uke*'s stomach.
- Sit back, bringing *uke*'s head down, lift up and over with your hands as you roll onto your back so *uke* rolls forward over your shoulder.

Daki wakare (high lift and separate)

This is normally used when *uke* has hands and feet on the ground after falling forward attempting a throw. It may not result in a high score, but you will be able to continue on the ground from a good position.

KEY POINTS
- Grab around *uke*'s waist from behind.
- Roll over *uke* to the right side.
- Hold tightly as you roll so you bring *uke* with you; *uke* rolls over you, landing to your left.

Kani basami (crab scissors)

Officially banned in tournaments after the Japanese champion, Yasuhiro Yamashita, was injured by this technique in a tournament leading up to the 1984 Olympic Games, this is nevertheless a strong, deceptive throw that is useful for self-defense.

KEY POINTS
- Pull your opponent upright and backwards, particularly with your right hand.
- Put your right leg in front of *uke*'s abdomen as your left leg goes behind *uke*'s knees (or lower).
- Scissor your legs and turn to the right, sweeping *uke*'s legs out and pulling *uke* backward.

Kawazu gake
(one-leg entanglement)

Kawazu gake is not permitted in judo competition or *randori* because of possible knee injuries. It involves wrapping your leg around your opponent's, sometimes called grapevining, and then falling backward on top of, or next to, *uke*. *Uke*'s leg is straightened and if you fall on it the knee may be hyperextended.

KEY POINTS:
- Slide your right leg between *uke*'s legs and wrap your foot around to the front of *uke*'s shin.
- Lift this trapped leg in front of you.
- Fall to your side or back, bringing *uke* down with you.

Uchi makikomi
(inner wraparound throw)

This is similar to *soto makikomi* (above) except that your right arm is under *uke*'s right arm rather than over it. The rolling throwing action is the same. This throw is often used after a failed *ippon seoinage* attempt when you are unable to lift *uke*.

KEY POINTS
- Enter your hips more deeply in front of *uke* than you would for *seoi nage*.
- Once *uke* is locked to your back, roll toward your right shoulder, bringing *uke* with you.

Osoto makikomi
(large outer wraparound)

This and the following *makikomi* throws rely on the principle of rotating your body while holding *uke*'s right arm tightly to you so that *uke*'s body is wrapped around yours like a cord around a spool. As you continue to wrap and fall, *uke* rolls over you and is brought down underneath you.

Osoto *makikomi* is used as a counter or follow-up to an *osoto gari* (page 00) attack.

KEY POINTS
- Attempt *osoto gari* and pull *uke* strongly with your left hand.
- *Uke*'s right arm must be wrapped well around your upper body so that *uke*'s shoulder is tight against your shoulder.
- Your twisting and rolling must be relentless; use your entire body weight to bring *uke* off balance and onto his back.

Soto makikomi
(outer wraparound throw)

This throw relies on strong rotation over your back, so your hips must enter deeply.

KEY POINTS
- Do not let your upper body separate from *uke*.
- Keep *uke*'s shoulder under your armpit as you roll forward.

Kouchi makikomi
(minor inner wraparound throw)

In *kouchi makikomi* you perform a throw similar to *kouchi gari* but enter your body deeply to prevent escape and provide power to this sacrifice throw. Instead of holding the lapel with your right hand, wrap your arm around the leg you are attacking, and use your right foot to hook and/or reap *uke*'s right foot. Place your right side into *uke*'s right hip and push to *uke*'s right rear corner until you land on top of *uke*.

In competition, *kouchi makikomi* must be applied without touching *uke*'s leg with your hand. This can be accomplished by pulling downward on *uke*'s right sleeve with both hands. It is often used in combination with *seoi nage*.

KEY POINTS
- Control *uke*'s right sleeve pulling down and to your left to pin *uke*'s weight onto the foot you are attacking.
- Focus on strongly pushing *uke*'s right hip with your forward body momentum while deeply hooking *uke*'s foot so that his weight falls behind his heel.
- By pushing *uke* back and maintaining close contact, *uke*'s right hip should land under you as you fall forward.

VARIATION
Grip variation for tournament

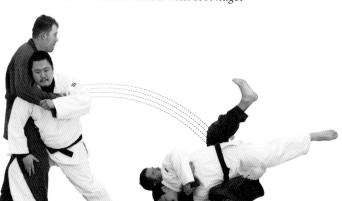

Uchi mata makikomi
(inner thigh wraparound)

After attempting an *uchi mata*, continue your forward pull directly into *uchi mata makikomi* by rolling forward and bringing yourself onto the ground, but with your opponent under you.

KEY POINTS
- The hand position is normally the same as in *soto makikomi* (opposite), but sometimes *uke*'s head is included in the grip.
- You will land directly on top of *uke*.

Harai makikomi
(sweeping wraparound)

After entering for *harai goshi*, continue your forward pull directly into *harai makikomi* by twisting to the left and rolling forward, bringing *uke* with you.

KEY POINTS
- Continue to pull powerfully with your left hand until you land on *uke*.
- Maintain tight body contact throughout the throw.

Hane makikomi
(springing wraparound throw)

After attacking with *hane goshi*, continue your forward pull directly into *hane makikomi* by twisting to your left, maintaining good contact and rolling forward.

KEY POINTS
- Your right hand may slip off *uke*'s head to increase your rotation.
- *Uke* should land directly under you as you roll forward.

GRAPPLING TECHNIQUES ON THE GROUND

Judo grappling techniques consist of pins, chokes, strangulations, arm locks and other joint locks. Many grappling techniques, particularly arm locks, can be performed either standing or on the ground, but pins are always used to immobilize an opponent on the mat. All grappling on the ground is called matwork, or *newaza*.

Whether you are training for competition or self-defense, you must master the basic positions of judo *newaza*, as well as transitions from standing techniques to ground techniques. The objective is to restrict your opponent's ability to escape, to dominate and exhaust them, and ultimately to force their surrender. At the same time you will be learning to defend yourself, to turn a bad position to your advantage, and to escape or counter attack.

Close combat on the ground can be intimidating for some, so start by getting used to grappling and pinning, then when you have some ability to control *uke*, expand your options with submissions. At first you may feel like resistance on the ground is futile, but as you learn how to apply judo grappling techniques more options will open up. Continued training allows you to improve on your weaknesses and to take advantage of your strengths to gain some control and turn the tables.

CHAPTER 1:
PINNING
(osaekomi waza)

The focus of *osaekomi waza* is to learn the basics of control and how to maintain a superior position on the ground. Knowing the final hold is only a small part of the skill needed to get an opponent into a vulnerable position, so other grappling situations must be studied as well. The pins and positions in this chapter are a small sample.

As you practice techniques on the ground, try to maintain a sense of fluidity by staying relaxed and using your strength to fullest advantage through leverage and balance. Yield to superior power and redirect it to your advantage. Maintain a stable base by keeping your center of gravity low. Strive to control at least one part of your opponent, then work to expand your control. Flexibility in applying technique is the key.

Basic grappling control: the hold down

Pinning skills are an important part of judo grappling because they teach you how to control an opponent, and conversely how to prevent or escape another person's control. These are essential lessons before moving on to strangulations or joint locks, where lack of control can lead to failure or injury. Pins are considered the basic control positions of judo grappling on the ground, and mastering the basics is always the key to success in more advanced studies.

In an ideal hold down, you should be able to safely control an opponent as long as necessary without hurting him or her. This gives you many self-defense options, including an opportunity to de-escalate a dangerous situation. Your pin may also be able to make an opponent submit from pressure, pain, exhaustion or suffocation. Finally, you can keep your opponent in a vulnerable position so you can apply more dangerous techniques, such as strikes or joint locks, if necessary.

Judo is like water

The nature of judo is often compared with that of water.

- Like judo *newaza*, water is the humblest of all the elements as it always seeks the low point, but in the end, it shows its power and overcomes by flowing around, over, or through an obstacle.
- Water is soft and follows the path of least resistance, always changing shape to fit the environment.
- Water is vital for life.
- It is highly adaptable: as serene as a lily pond or as wild as the stormy sea, solid as ice or vaporous as steam, clear as a mountain stream or as murky as fog.
- It can suddenly split rocks when freezing, or wear them down with constant attacks one drop at a time.
- Water is most serviceable to life when in its liquid state; judo is most effective when your technique is applied in a fluid manner.
- Remember that when water and fire wage war, water will always be the victor.
- Water covers most of the earth yet its vast depths are largely unexplored.

Hal Sharp (1927–2021), renowned judoka and author of numerous judo books and videos, used to say that a solid pin should be so tight that your opponent won't be able to move anything but their eyeballs. When applied properly without any weakness for an opponent to exploit, the end is inevitable.

Pinning techniques allow you to easily control someone from a superior top position because you can bear all your weight down onto the helpless subject stuck on his back. This conserves your energy, tires your opponent, and gives you various options, including applying greater force if needed. But when holding a pin, you are also generally free to get up at any time. Pins can be among the gentlest skills in judo, yet they are very effective for protecting yourself in many situations, and for subduing an adversary when necessary.

What is a pin?

A pin in judo is a control hold that keeps your opponent on his back and prevents him from rising. For a pin to count in competition it must be applied from above (that is, you must be on top to put pressure on *uke*). You cannot be between your opponent's legs (guard position), or have one of your legs controlled by your opponent (half guard). Your position may be face down (as in *kami shiho gatame*), face up (as in *ura gatame*), upright (as in *uki gatame*), or on your side (as in *kesa gatame*). It is never allowed to hold a pin just around the head/neck (as in a headlock) without control of at least one arm.

To score a winning point (*ippon*) in a tournament you must maintain control and prevent escape for 20 seconds (or until the opponent submits). Judo competition statistics show that very few contestants can escape from a pin if they cannot do so within the first 20 seconds. A smaller score is awarded for a hold of shorter duration: at least 10, but less than 20, seconds scores *waza ari* (near *ippon*).

Each pinning technique has multiple variations. The term for a modified hold, or variation, is *kuzure*, so *kuzure kesa gatame* is a modified version of the *kesa gatame*. There are ten ways of pinning recognized by the Kodokan (since two were added in 2017). Although each pin is easily recognized, there are many ways to apply them with different grips or modified positions while maintaining the basic principle of the original pin.

Principles

Balance is a key component of success in pinning, as it is in standing judo. The basic principle of *kuzushi* (unbalancing the opponent) that permits a throw to work easily is just as important on the ground. When you stand with two feet on the ground, you are easily moved and your balance is naturally more precarious, although your freedom of movement allows you to regain balance quickly. When you are on the ground you generally have less freedom to move but better balance, and it is sometimes more difficult to be aware of your balance or to control your opponent's. This is one of the reasons Jigoro Kano emphasized standing techniques as a means for teaching the secrets of *kuzushi*. Once learned, your sense of balance and skills in off-balancing can help dramatically on the ground.

In every pin try to keep a wide base (e.g. legs spread), stay as low as possible, keep as much weight as you can on your opponent, and move your body in a relaxed manner to respond to your opponent's actions. The opposite is true when trying to escape. To escape, try to restrict or take advantage of your opponent's movement, get your opponent's center of gravity off his or her base, get your opponent as high as possible off the ground, and make your opponent's base as small as possible.

When you are on the bottom, space is your friend; when you are on top, it is your enemy. To prevent a pin or escape from it, create as much space as possible between you and an opponent. Conversely, to pin someone, remove any space between you. When you are on top, get as close as possible to the opponent so you can effectively apply your weight and restrict the opponent's movement.

In addition to learning how to use each pin to maintain control, it is important to study the methods of finding and exploiting the weaknesses of each pin so that you can escape. The best escapes start long before you are pinned; you must prevent your opponent from getting a better position than you. Once a pin is successfully locked on, the person on top has a clear advantage that can only be overcome with superior skill. An immediate defense or counterattack is needed before your opponent gains complete control.

A strong pin establishes the control needed to apply arm locks or other submissions.

Kesa gatame (scarf hold)

This is called the scarf hold because you wrap yourself around *uke*'s head and body like a sash. You should be able to hold someone without much effort when you have the right position. Try to remain relaxed and fluid so you can respond easily to your opponent's attempts to escape. Also practice applying this technique as quickly as possible after throwing so that your opponent does not have the opportunity to prevent you from getting the strong position you want.

Kesa gatame can also be applied to make it difficult for your opponent to breathe. Encircle *uke*'s right arm around your torso as you lean forward and grab high on the arm. Hold it tightly and rotate your body so *uke*'s right arm is pulled up and your body is pushed heavily onto *uke*'s chest to compress the lungs.

KEY POINTS
- Keep control of *uke*'s arm and wrap it tightly around your body.
- Keep your legs spread for a solid base.
- Keep your head down, and control *uke*'s head by keeping it off the mat.

Ushiro kesa gatame
(reverse scarf hold)

Ushiro kesa gatame is similar to *kesa gatame* except it is applied by facing the other direction – towards *uke*'s feet rather than *uke*'s head. Place your far arm under *uke*'s far shoulder and try to grab the belt (or jacket). Control *uke*'s near arm as in *kesa gatame* by keeping the elbow off the mat and squeezing the arm tightly under your armpit.

KEY POINTS
- Apply your weight across the upper chest of your opponent.
- Restrict *uke*'s movement by holding your opponent tightly against your hip, controlling both shoulders.
- Lean forward, keep your head down, and keep your legs well spread to prevent the most common bridging escapes.

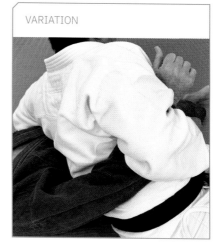

VARIATION

Kuzure kesa gatame

(modified scarf hold)

This pin looks very much like *kesa gatame*, but with a variation. Instead of placing one arm around the head, your arm should be placed on the mat under your opponent's far-side arm. This position is conducive to easily switch between pins (or apply an effective armlock), and it prevents your opponent from escaping by pushing your arm off the head.

KEY POINTS

- Keep tight control over the arm you are holding (*uke*'s right arm in the photo).
- Respond to your partner's escape attempts by flattening *uke* onto his back, pulling up on *uke*'s arm, and raising *uke*'s head to prevent bridging.
- Apply your weight to control *uke*'s shoulder and upper body.

VARIATION

VARIATION
Makura kesa gatame

Kata gatame (shoulder hold)

This can be applied as both a pin and a strangulation that forces your opponent to submit. To apply the strangulation, drive your weight down onto *uke*'s arm, which is then pressed into *uke*'s own neck. Your own arm around *uke*'s neck squeezes to complete the strangulation on both sides of the neck.

KEY POINTS
- Hold *uke*'s head tightly to prevent movement or escape.
- Keep your head against *uke*'s head so *uke*'s arm cannot slip out.
- Drive your shoulder into *uke*'s neck while squeezing with your arm.

VARIATION

Kami shiho gatame

(top four-corner hold)

This is a strong pin because you are on top of *uke*'s chest from above his head, so his legs cannot be used effectively to escape. Reach under *uke*'s shoulders to grab the belt and pull *uke* in tightly.

KEY POINTS
- Hang on tightly to *uke*'s belt with your hands.
- Keep your legs spread apart to form a strong base.
- Keep your hips low and maintain your weight on your opponent while keeping in line with *uke*.

Kuzure kami shiho gatame
(modified top four-corner hold)

Kuzure kami shiho gatame is a modified *kami shiho gatame* where you change the position of the right hand to grab inside the collar behind *uke's* head. To apply this pin from above *uke's* head, reach over *uke's* arm then under the shoulder to the collar grip. Place your fingers inside the collar and bring your hand to the mat. Your right shoulder should be on top of *uke's* shoulder trapping it in place.

Uki gatame (floating hold)

Your opponent is on his back and you are in position to apply *juji gatame* – you are sitting next to *uke* with one leg over his chest and one leg over his neck with his nearest arm under your control. When he prevents the armbar by locking his arms together, remove your leg nearest his head and put it behind you so you can push forward and put your weight on *uke*. Continue to control the arm so that when he attempts an escape you can maintain the pin or return to the armlock.

A second version involves placing your knee on *uke's* abdomen while holding a lapel and the near arm. In both cases you are not completely straddling *uke*, but one leg is applying the pressure to keep the opponent down.

Ura gatame (back pin)

Place your back on your opponent's chest so that you are facing up. Wrap one arm around his neck (or control the nearest arm) and wrap the other arm around one or both legs. With your feet flat on the mat, bridge up slightly to apply all your weight on your opponent flattening him and making it difficult to move.

Yoko shiho gatame
(side four-corner hold)

In this side-control hold, your chest pushes down on *uke*'s chest to keep *uke*'s back flat on the mat. Variations include *kuzure yoko shiho gatame* (modified side four-corner hold) and *mune gatame* (chest hold). Your objective should be to stay on *uke*'s chest with your legs at a right angle perpendicular to your opponent in order to prevent *uke*'s arm or leg from grabbing and gaining control over your legs.

KEY POINTS
- Reach around *uke*'s far leg to grab the belt, jacket, arm, or pants, while the other hand reaches around *uke*'s neck to grab the collar or shoulder.
- Keep your legs spread apart to form a strong base.
- Keep your hips low and make sure you keep maximum pressure on your opponent's chest.

VARIATION
Mune gatame

VARIATION
Kuzure yoko shiho gatame (1)

VARIATION
Kuzure yoko shiho gatame (2)

Tate shiho gatame
(straight four-corner hold)

Mount your opponent with one leg on each side as you sit on *uke*'s abdomen. Hand and foot positions can vary and all variations are called *kuzure tate shiho gatame* (modified straight four-corner hold). Since your body is higher than *uke*'s and your legs are not spread as far as in most pins, keeping your balance requires greater skill. This pin is important for self-defense as you can control *uke* with your legs, freeing your hands to strike if necessary.

KEY POINTS
- Keep your knees spread as much as possible to widen your base and put downward pressure on *uke*.
- Control *uke*'s hips with your legs.
- Keep your arms relaxed so you can post them on the mat to stop *uke*'s attempts to roll you off.

VARIATION
Variation of arm position

Basic foot position

VARIATION
Variation of foot position

VARIATION
Variation of foot position

Basic ground positions

When both opponents are on the ground, four important positions must be mastered. One person will be either on his back (face up) or stomach (face down), with the opponent on top. From each position, whether you are on top or bottom, you must learn to take the initiative. Trying to maintain your position defensively will only yield the opportunity to your opponent for a variety of attacks, so always work towards improving your position. When transitioning from throws to *newaza* try to maintain control so that you land in a favorable position.

YOU ARE FACE DOWN – BOTTOM POSITION

A general rule in grappling martial arts is never to turn your back on your opponent. When you are face down on the ground, you are vulnerable to attack. If you are unavoidably on the ground face down with your opponent over you, first try to protect yourself by getting on your hands and knees (or elbows and knees). This is primarily a defensive position used in competition to avoid a pinning technique, to gain mobility, or to help your efforts to stand up. This position should only be used as a transition between lying face down on the mat and standing up, reversing the positions, or while turning to face your opponent to initiate an attack. Offensive options for the person on the bottom are much more limited than for the one on top, so the longer you stay in this position the more likely you will be defeated.

YOUR OPPONENT IS FACE DOWN – TOP POSITION

The hands and knees position in judo is sometimes called the turtle position, because a defensive contestant may pull his or her arms in to protect from arm locks and cover the neck to protect from chokes. In judo tournaments you will only have a short opportunity to begin to break down the turtle position and you must demonstrate steady progress towards a successful technique. Your attacks must thus be drilled repeatedly against resisting opponents so you can create immediate progress. There are many ways to attack the turtle position with turnovers that lead to pins, arm locks and chokes. Another option is to gain control from the back so you can apply arm locks, chokes or strangulations from the rear.

YOU ARE FACE UP – BOTTOM POSITION

The guard position is when you are lying on your back with your opponent kneeling or standing between your legs. This may result in a stalemate, with neither contestant able to establish enough control to apply a pin, arm lock or choke. The person on the bottom uses his legs to control the top person and prevent attacks, while attempting to turn him over to gain a superior position. The person who is between the legs must try to get out from the legs so as to attack freely.

Once in this position in a judo tournament, the referee will only permit a short time for either contestant to make progress towards greater control. Although this position is primarily defensive for the person on the bottom, against a less skilled opponent it can easily become offensive since you can successfully attack in many ways, for instance, by sweeping out your opponent's legs to get on top, or applying an arm lock from the bottom, such as *ude hishigi juji gatame* or *ude garami*.

When you are on your back with an opponent beside you, use your legs to gain control of your opponent before he or she secures a pin or uses another technique.

To defend against an opponent approaching from the right, immediately bring your right knee and elbow together in a position often called the shrimp. As you bring your knee and elbow in to block your opponent's advance, slide your hips away to create more space. This should provide the opportunity to wrap your legs around at least part of your opponent – and in this way begin the process of gaining control.

One common rule of self-defense when you are on your back is always to keep your legs between yourself and your opponent. If your attacker begins to get around your legs, you need to continually push him back down to your legs while moving your upper body away. Your legs are much stronger than your arms, and can be used to keep an opponent further away since they are also longer.

When you are on your back protecting yourself from an attack, your defensive objective should always be to keep as much space as possible between you and your opponent. When you have sufficient confidence to begin an attack from your back, you will want to control the space between you and your opponent and at that point you can begin to close the distance.

YOUR OPPONENT IS FACE UP – TOP POSITION

The person on top (between the legs) can also use various methods to escape and gain complete control. In this case, gravity is on your side and you can apply your weight onto your opponent. The more you lean onto your opponent, however, the less solid your base is, so be careful to keep your center of gravity low to prevent yourself from being rolled over. In general, keep your head higher than your hips and as much over your hips as you can, with your legs spread for a wide base. For every attempt you make at escaping the legs, your opponent has defenses and attacks, so try to keep your balance at all times as you try to improve your position. Focus on getting better control before attempting submissions.

Tips for groundfighting

Movement should be fluid and natural.

Maintain a wide, low base for stability.

Utilize your weight to your advantage.

Keep your arms close to your body.

Always face your opponent.

Keep your head over your hips to maintain balance.

Use your feet like extra hands.

CHAPTER 2:
STRANGULATION AND CHOKING
(shime waza)

Choking and strangulation are subtle techniques that require more attention to detail than most other judo skills because the targets are usually small, specific areas of the neck that are often well protected by your opponent. Accuracy, not brute strength, is the key.

In some chokes the hands use the lapel as if it were a thin cord to encircle the throat; in others they twist or rotate powerfully into the neck; in yet others they pull or push to apply pressure directly to the carotid arteries or trachea (windpipe). Finally, some chokes do not use the arms at all and the pressure is applied by the legs. You can apply even the basic chokes effectively in multiple ways, depending on the position, relative size and movement of your opponent, as well as your training, strengths and preferences.

The chokes shown here are examples of the standard position for the twelve techniques recognized by the Kodokan intended to assist in learning the principle involved, but they do not show all the variations or positions in which each technique can be applied. Your study of chokes is not complete without training multiple ways to enter into each *shime waza*, how to escape and defend chokes, how to overcome defenses to apply your choke, and transitions between various *shime waza*, pins, armlocks, throws, turnovers, guard escapes, etc. In addition to the standard chokes there are also other applications of *shime waza*, including pins (like *kata gatame*), pin escapes, turnovers, etc.

Principles

There are two primary ways for *shime waza* to cause a submission or unconsciousness of an opponent, as well as some combinations of the two:

- stopping or restricting the flow of blood to the brain: i.e. compressing the carotid arteries on one or both sides of the neck;
- stopping or reducing the flow of air to the lungs: i.e. directly compressing the trachea, blocking the mouth to keep the victim from inhaling (suffocation), or restricting the diaphragm and/or lungs to prevent the opponent from inhaling (often used during pinning techniques or directly with the legs as in *do jime*).

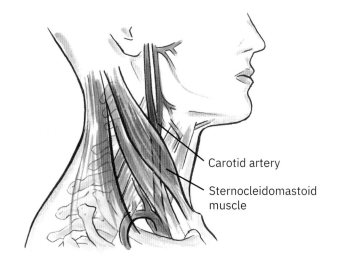

Carotid artery

Sternocleidomastoid muscle

Anatomy of a choke

Top tips for effective strangulation

A good strangulation hold should render any opponent unconscious without injury or significant pain – in a matter of seconds. Here are the basic requirements.

- Ensure your own body has complete freedom of action so you are in the best position for the technique you intend to use, and you are flexible enough to respond to *uke*'s attempts to escape. Your position should be stable so you can use the power of your entire body, not just your hands.

- Lead *uke* into a position in which it is most difficult to put up resistance, and control all *uke*'s actions. *Uke* must be unstable, off balance and under your control as much as possible. Often this means stretching or straightening out *uke*'s body.

- Train your hands to get an accurate hold the moment you begin a technique, and make it work quickly. Once you begin the pressure, do not continually release to adjust your position. Firmly resolve not to let your opponent get away, but to continue until the end without slackening. Constant pressure is called for rather than extreme force. Excessive reliance on strength suggests defective technique since very little pressure is needed to compress an artery and render someone unconscious.

Attacks on the neck are sometimes distinguished by a variety of terms and may be referred to as choking, strangling, wringing or neck locks. However, they are grouped together as a class of grappling techniques called *shime waza*. *Shime* means constriction and *waza* means technique. The term 'choking' technically refers to a blockage of the windpipe or mouth that prevents breathing, whereas strangulation means compression of the arteries in the neck to prevent blood from reaching the brain, but it is common in judo to use the word 'choke' for all *shime waza*.

Practice all types of chokes as they are useful for various situations, but strangulation is generally stressed in most judo classes around the world. Compression of the carotid arteries is the most important form of *shime waza* because it requires the least force so it is most in keeping with the efficiency principle of judo – maximum effect with minimum effort. It is also the quickest way to produce unconsciousness and the most universally effective against various types and sizes of opponents.

Medical tests have established that the amount of pressure needed to block the arteries in strangulation is six times less than that required to choke someone by collapsing the airway. Directly stopping the blood supply to the brain also results in loss of consciousness at least six times faster than indirectly reducing oxygen in the brain through restricting breathing or the flow of air to the lungs.

Carotid strangulations are safer and involve less pain than other most other *shime waza* methods, which makes them more compatible with another basic principle of judo – mutual welfare and benefit. These techniques are easier to practice so it possible to acquire sufficient skill to gain confidence in using them. A skillfully executed technique enables you to produce unconsciousness or submission with little pain or forewarning to your opponent. This makes it a powerful weapon in judo's arsenal of techniques.

Even though chokes and strangulations are extremely effective against unskilled opponents, only a small percentage of international judo contests are won with the use of *shime waza*. This is primarily because of various effective defenses. Just as studying throws improves your balance and makes you harder to throw, training in *shime waza* should increase your awareness of vulnerabilities to chokes and strangles, and improve your ability to avoid or withstand such attacks.

The most important defensive rule is to keep your chin down and your shoulders up, so the target – your neck – is inaccessible to your opponent. Your hands can also protect your neck. Be aware of your opponent's attempts to grip your *judogi* in a way that enables a *shime waza* technique. For example, do not let your opponent get a grip high on your collar, or once this grip is secured, keep control of the other hand so it cannot finish the strangulation.

One unique aspect of *shime waza* techniques is that they can be applied from behind your opponent. To prevent this, never give your opponent your back or let your opponent get control of you from behind. If this does happen, immediately protect your neck while attempting to escape.

Safety

Shime waza must be taught and supervised by a qualified instructor. Since the judo syllabus has always contained more well-developed strangulation and choking techniques than

most other martial arts, judo instructors usually have extensive experience with proper application. *Shime waza* are potentially dangerous and should be treated seriously. As taught in judo, though, they are temporary incapacitating techniques of short duration whose proper execution should be harmless. *Shime waza* have been used in judo classes and tournaments around the world for more than 120 years without a single reported fatality. Only with appropriate emphasis on safety and supervision can this record be maintained.

Care should be taken when teaching *shime waza* to children, whose physiology is less developed than adults'. In most judo tournaments chokes are not permitted for young children. Children over the permissible age may learn basic *shime waza* with escapes and defenses, but always under strict supervision. For children – and beginners of any age – the emphasis should be on recognizing the effect of chokes or strangles, and protecting yourself while avoiding extreme pressure and unconsciousness in practice.

Shime waza may be practiced from either a standing position or on the ground, but the ground is inherently safer. When applying a standing *shime waza* with the intention of gaining the full effect, the victim will not be able to remain standing. In tournament and practice the person being strangled should always be taken to the ground immediately for better control and to prevent an accidental fall that could injure an opponent who becomes unconscious.

To avoid unnecessary periods of unconsciousness, learning when to submit is an important part of training. While you should not give up an opportunity to escape from *shime waza*, you must surrender once you recognize defeat is inevitable and further resistance will cause unconsciousness. Once you allow yourself to be choked unconscious your life is literally in your opponent's hands, and the practice of any martial art requires you to learn ways of avoiding this ultimate helplessness. Since it is virtually impossible to speak while being choked, the universal signal for submission is repeatedly

Defenses for the following three cross chokes

- Keep your chin down on your chest while shrugging your shoulders high.

- Keep *uke* from getting a deep grip or pulling you in because the further away *uke* is, the less effective the strangulation. A simple defense is to put both hands on your opponent's chest and push away while posturing up to create space (watch out for an armbar). Your legs may also keep *uke* away in some positions like the guard.

- Before your opponent gets a grip with both hands, grab high on your own lapel or place the palm of your hand on your cheek or neck so that your hand protects your neck and is in the way of the strangulation.

- Separate your opponent's arms by pushing the elbow on top up, while pushing the one underneath down. This will effectively uncross his arms to weaken the choke and allow your head to escape.

- Often, moving one direction tightens the choke and moving the other direction loosens it. If you have mobility try shifting your body in the direction that uncrosses the arms and relieves the pressure.

- Use both hands to sharply pull your own lapel down to free it or allow you to get your chin down.

tapping the opponent or mat.

The most important safety rule for *shime waza* is to release pressure immediately after the opponent submits or begins to feel the effect of the technique. You should be sensitive enough – and have sufficient control – to recognize when *uke* begins to lose consciousness so that you can immediately release pressure even if *uke* does not tap. Loss of consciousness can be detected easily by sudden lack of resistance, the generally limp feeling of *uke*'s body, and perhaps a change in the color of the face, spasms, or other signs.

Nami juji jime (normal cross lock)

The first three strangulations are all called cross locks (*juji* means cross) because of the crossed position of your arms as you wring *uke*'s neck. They are similar in principle and appearance, though the exact position of the hands varies. The changes in hand position influence the ways each technique can be used.

For *nami juji jime*, cross your arms and grab *uke*'s collar high on each side of the neck. Place your thumbs inside the *judogi* so your palms face down. To apply strangulation, spread your elbows apart and up, wrapping your hands around *uke*'s neck. By hanging on tightly to the collar, the sides of your hands will roll the protective muscle forward and press on the carotid artery located on each side of *uke*'s neck. The pressure on the trachea should be minimal.

KEY POINTS
- From the front, grab high on the collar, with thumbs in and arms crossed.
- Spread your elbows and expand your chest as you pull on the collar.
- Bring your hands (and your partner) close to your chest.

VARIATION
Application from the rear

Gyaku juji jime (reverse cross lock)

This is similar to *nami juji jime* except your hands are reversed so that your palms are up and your fingers are inside *uke*'s collar. This strangle is also applied by spreading your elbows and drawing your hands around the neck, though a different part of your hands will now compress the target arteries. To increase the effectiveness of this strangle, or to use the technique when *uke* is defending well and you cannot draw *uke* close, rotate your hands. Hold the collar firmly; try to turn your hands so that the palms face down and the knife edge of your hand will be pressed into both sides of *uke*'s neck.

KEY POINTS
- From the front, grab high on the collar, with your thumbs out and arms crossed.
- Spread your elbows and expand your chest as you pull on the collar.
- Draw your opponent close to increase the effectiveness of the choke.

VARIATION
Application from the bottom

Kata juji jime (half cross lock)

This is also similar to *nami juji jime* except that one hand grabs high on *uke*'s collar with the thumb in, while your other arm crosses under the first and you grab lower on the opposite collar or lapel with your fingers inside the *judogi*. The choking action comes primarily from your top hand on the collar wrapping around *uke*'s neck, while the other hand anchors the lapel down. The side of your choking hand applies pressure as in *nami juji jime*.

KEY POINTS
- From the front, grab high on the collar, with your thumb in the judogi.
- With your other hand, grab the opposite lapel, with your fingers in; pull down.
- Bring your head and chest close to *uke* as you bring the hand on the collar around *uke*'s neck in a circular manner.

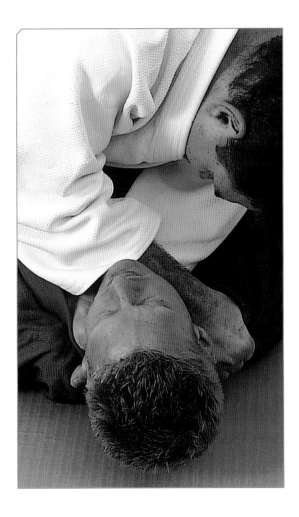

Application from standing

Hadaka jime (naked lock)

This is called the naked lock because you do not use the *judogi* to apply the choking action as in other *shime waza*. Place your arm across the throat from behind your opponent to apply pressure directly to the trachea. This prevents breathing, and can be very painful; usually your opponent will give up from the pain long before the choke takes effect. There are several variations of the basic choke, including versions that compress the arteries like other strangulations (sleeper holds).

KEY POINTS
- Put *uke* into an off-balance position where you can control *uke*'s movement.
- Place the inside edge of your forearm or wrist against *uke*'s throat so that your palm is down.
- Place your shoulder behind *uke*'s head, and your head against the side of *uke*'s head, to control it.

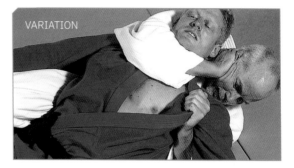

Kataha jime (single wing lock)

This is applied from the rear like *okuri eri jime* except your left hand does not grab *uke's* lapel. While your right hand strangles or chokes *uke*, your left hand controls *uke*'s head and left arm, making it difficult for *uke* to relieve the pressure on the neck or turn out of the *shime waza*.

KEY POINTS
- Grab *uke*'s left lapel with your right hand across *uke*'s throat, controlling *uke*'s left arm with your left forearm.
- Slide your left hand to a position directly behind *uke*'s head or neck, usually with the back of your left hand against the base of *uke*'s head.
- *Uke's* left arm should be pointing up over *uke*'s head as you apply the strangulation or choke.

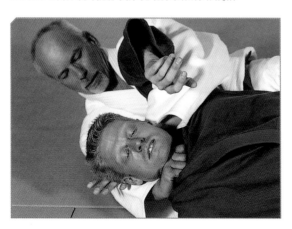

Okuri eri jime (sliding collar lock)

Another strangle from the rear, this uses the lapel like a cord wrapped around *uke's* neck. In addition to the constricting action of the lapel, the inside edge of your right wrist or forearm compresses the carotid artery on one side of the neck. It can also be used as a choke, with the inside edge of your right forearm or wrist applying pressure directly on the trachea. Try to straighten *uke's* body to weaken defenses and maintain control, then use the power of your body (expanding your chest, arching your back, thrusting your hips forward) to assist the choke.

KEY POINTS
- Put *uke* in an off-balance position completely under your control so *uke* cannot turn or curl up.
- Use your left hand to reach under *uke's* left arm to grab *uke's* right lapel, and pull it down towards *uke's* waist.
- Pull *uke's* left lapel around *uke's* neck with your right hand.

VARIATION

A variation used as a counter to seoi nage

Katate jime (one-hand choke)

One common version is similar to *kata juji jime* except only one hand applies the choke without the assistance of the other hand. It can be performed from a variety of pins or positions, but the key element is that only one hand applies the choke.

KEY POINTS
- Immobilize *uke* completely.
- Grab *uke*'s lapel with one hand, with your thumb inside the *judogi*.
- Bring your elbow around *uke*'s throat, applying pressure directly on the trachea with your forearm.

Ryote jime (two-hand choke)

Here you apply pressure with your knuckles directly onto the area of the carotid arteries to stop the flow of blood to the brain.

KEY POINTS
- Grab *uke*'s collar with both hands, one on each side.
- Get your thumbs inside the collar, approximately under *uke*'s ears.
- Pull with both hands and rotate your knuckles into each side of *uke*'s neck as you turn your palms upward.

VARIATION

Sode guruma jime
(sleeve wheel choke)

This is applied by gripping your own *judogi* to apply leverage into *uke*'s throat. It is most successful when you have control of *uke* between your legs from either the top or the bottom.

KEY POINTS
- Place your left forearm behind *uke*'s head and grab *uke*'s collar or shoulder, or your own sleeve.
- Grab your own left sleeve with your right hand.
- Bring the outside edge of your right forearm down across *uke*'s throat in a circular motion.

Tsukkomi jime (thrust choke)

This works by thrusting your knuckles directly into the side of your opponent's neck. It may be applied as either a choke or strangulation, depending on the placement of your knuckles and how you use your opponent's lapel.

KEY POINTS
- Grab *uke*'s left lapel with your right hand (thumb inside the *judogi*).
- Grip *uke*'s right lapel with your left hand (fingers inside the *judogi*, palm facing down).
- Pull with your right hand as you push your left hand directly into the side of *uke*'s neck, pulling the lapel across *uke*'s throat.

Sankaku jime (triangle choke)

This is a powerful choke that multiplies the strength of your legs and hips through leverage. Your legs make a triangle shape by placing one foot behind the knee of your other leg. Inside the triangle is the neck and one shoulder of your opponent. Your hands may assist the choke, but the primary action is from your legs which constrict the neck. It can be performed from the front, side, back, above or below your opponent.

KEY POINTS
- Trap *uke*'s head and one arm between your legs.
- Place one foot behind the knee of your other leg.
- Bend your knee to tighten the choke as you pinch your knees together.

Do jime (body scissors or trunk choke)

This is another powerful choke that utilizes the strength of your legs and hips, but the principle is different from other chokes because the pressure is not applied to the neck at all. *Do jime* involves using your legs in the guard position to forcibly squeeze your opponent's trunk to prevent breathing and obtain a submission. *Do jime* is not permitted in judo competition due to the incidence of injury caused by its forceful application.

KEY POINTS
- Lock your feet together to give maximum leverage.
- Pull *uke*'s head down to further restrict breathing and prevent escape.
- Straighten your legs to bring your knees close together forcefully squeezing *uke*.

CHAPTER 3:
JOINT LOCKS
(kansetsu waza)

Joint locks involve manipulating an opponent's joints by twisting, stretching, separating or bending in any direction beyond their normal range. The aim is to compel an adversary to surrender because of pain from the beginning of a sprain or dislocation of the joint, particularly the elbow. If applied quickly and forcefully, joint locks can result in various injuries from a mild sprain to more serious torn ligaments, dislocations, or even broken bones.

Although attacks against all joints were permitted in early judo contests, for safety reasons joint locks have gradually been restricted in tournaments to the elbow only. In 1899, locks of the fingers, toes, wrists, and ankles were banned. Knee entanglement or twisting knee locks were banned in 1916. Joint lock attacks were limited in contests to the elbow only in 1925 because of the severity of injuries resulting from attacking other joints with full force in contests.

Elbow joint locks have proven relatively safe as the opponent has ample opportunity to tap before injury can occur. They can be carefully practiced in *randori* and tournaments without serious risk. Learning locks on the elbow helps in understanding all joint locks, but further study of joint locks against the knee, ankle, wrist, fingers and spine is preserved in judo *kata*. There are ten joint locks recognized by the Kodokan (nine arm locks and one knee lock).

Principles

Modern arm locks aim to apply pressure to the elbow in one of two basic ways:

- The bent arm lock, *ude garami*.
- The straight arm lock (or arm bar), for example *ude hishigi ude gatame*.

In both cases the key requirement is to control *uke*'s body so *uke* cannot escape by moving. You must specifically control the shoulder, elbow and wrist of the arm being attacked. To apply leverage against the elbow, you normally immobilize the shoulder and then apply pressure against the wrist and the elbow in opposite directions to force submission or, if necessary, to dislocate the arm.

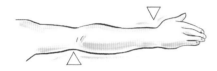

Leverage in straight arm bars creates more force than the joint can withstand.

Some arm locks can create tremendous force on the joint by utilizing all of your body, especially the hips, to apply pressure to the elbow. However, exact placement of the pressure on the fulcrum of the lever (the elbow) is essential for maximum efficiency, particularly against a stronger opponent. The fulcrum should generally be placed at the hollow just above the point of the elbow. You can feel this spot if you straighten your arm, place your finger on the point of the bone, then slide it towards your shoulder a few centimetres.

The most powerful arm bars use your entire body to apply pressure to the joint.

The exact position of the wrist is also important for skillful application of arm locks. In straight arm locks, pressure on the wrist should ideally be applied towards the little finger, away from the thumb. This makes it much more difficult for your opponent to turn out and escape from the arm bar.

Safety

Joint locks must be taught and supervised by a qualified instructor as they are potentially dangerous. Once you gain sufficient control over your opponent, you should be able to apply the technique with precision, providing opportunity for your opponent to signal defeat by tapping. In most practice and tournaments, arm locks are not permitted for children since their bones are not yet fully developed. They are more susceptible to seri-ous injury when practising because they lack experience and maturity. For children and beginners of all ages the emphasis should be on safety to guarantee years of healthy judo practice.

Arm locks may be practiced from either a standing position or on the ground, but the ground is usually safer. The victim of your arm lock can move around more freely when standing than on the ground. Since you have less control over an opponent's movement when he is standing, you may have to apply the technique more quickly for success and there is a greater likelihood of injury. In practice, take your opponent to the ground for better control and to prevent an accident.

The universal signal for submission is tapping the opponent or mat repeatedly. Learning when to tap is important to avoid risk of injury. Do not forfeit any opportunity to escape from arm locks, but surrender when further resistance will lead to injury. Arm locks usually hurt, but this varies from person to person, so proper training about the elbow's vulnerability to dislocation helps prevent injury.

The most important safety rule for arm locks is to release pressure immediately when the opponent signals defeat by tapping. You should have sufficient control over your opponent to recognize when the lock takes effect, so you can release pressure before injury even if *uke* does not tap. Once an arm is extended to the limit of its range of motion, *uke*'s ability to resist is greatly diminished so you must make sure that your application of pressure is careful and measured.

Ude garami (entangled arm lock)

This popular bent-arm lock can be applied from many different positions – standing, from a pin or from underneath *uke*. The angle of the arm you are attacking must be bent, with the hand pointing either up above *uke*'s head, or down towards *uke*'s feet. In different variations of this technique you may push *uke*'s hand away from you, pull *uke*'s elbow towards you, bring *uke*'s hand in towards *uke*'s shoulder, or a combination of movements.

This arm lock can be used to apply pressure on *uke*'s shoulder, potentially separating or dislocating it. This is useful when standing to force *uke* to the ground, or when on the ground to roll *uke* over. With additional study and greater skill, the pressure can be applied on the elbow, and you will be able to dislocate it if necessary.

KEY POINTS

- Gain control over *uke*'s movement, and immobilize *uke*'s shoulder.
- Grab *uke*'s wrist so the back of your hand is towards you, and the thumb side of your hand is towards the elbow you are attacking.
- Place your other forearm behind *uke*'s elbow, then grab your own wrist. The back of your hand should be facing towards you.
- Maintain pressure on the elbow and slide it towards *uke*'s waist.

VARIATION

VARIATION

VARIATION

VARIATION

Ude hishigi juji gatame

(cross arm lock)

Commonly called *juji gatame*, this cross arm lock gets its name from your position across your opponent's body. One of the most effective arm locks in judo, it is consistently the number-one winning arm lock used in international judo competition. It is a specialty of the 1981 World Champion, Neil Adams, of the Great Britain. It is equally effective in high-level competition and in self-defense, and is included in many modern and traditional jujutsu systems. It is particularly powerful because you use your entire body, including the strength of the legs and hips, to control *uke* and apply tremendous pressure to the straightened arm. For this reason it can be used easily against larger or stronger opponents.

KEY POINTS
- Control *uke*'s wrist with your hands so the little finger side of *uke*'s hand is against your chest.
- Control *uke*'s shoulder by squeezing your knees together, and control *uke*'s body with your legs.
- Keep *uke*'s elbow around your hips or abdomen, and bridge your body (raise the hips) if necessary to apply pressure on the elbow.

APPLICATION
Following a throw

VARIATION
Gyaku juji gatame

Ude hishigi hiza gatame

(knee arm lock)

Hiza gatame is used in the *Katame no Kata* by forcing *uke* face down on the ground. By straightening your opponent's arm and using your knee to apply downward pressure on the elbow you can prevent escape and make *uke* submit.

KEY POINTS
- Hold *uke*'s wrist with your hands and stretch *uke*'s arm straight.
- Put your foot on *uke*'s hip for leverage and control.
- Place your knee on top of *uke*'s elbow and push down.

VARIATION

Ude hishigi ude gatame

(straight arm lock)

Ude gatame is a simple, direct arm lock that can be applied while standing to bring an opponent down, or on the ground to force submission. Although it looks simple, exact placement and body control are needed to make it effective against a resisting opponent.

KEY POINTS

- Use your head to trap *uke*'s hand or wrist on your shoulder.
- Cup both hands on the point of the elbow.
- Focusing the pressure on the little-finger side of your hands, force *uke*'s straightened arm into hyperextension.

VARIATION
Standing

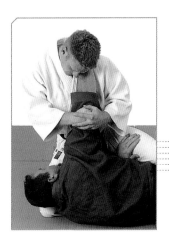

Ude hishigi waki gatame

(armpit arm lock)

Waki gatame is a strong lock that uses your own body weight against *uke*'s elbow joint. When attempting this from a standing position, be careful to give your opponent an opportunity to tap – fast and forceful execution can result in injury. It is useful for self-defense, and can be effective against an opponent who is stiff-arming you to keep you away.

KEY POINTS

- With both hands, grip *uke*'s wrist so your thumbs are close to *uke*'s hand.
- Place your right elbow over *uke*'s arm so your shoulder is just above *uke*'s elbow joint.
- Gain control of *uke*'s shoulder by forcing it to the ground, then lean on the elbow and lift *uke*'s hand to apply pressure on the elbow.

VARIATION
Gyaku waki gatame

Ude hishigi hara gatame

(stomach arm lock)

Hara is the place in your abdomen where your center of gravity is when you are upright. Traditionally considered in Eastern thought to be the seat of the soul and the center of *ki*, or life force, it is located just below your navel. This part of your body is used directly against the elbow joint in *hara gatame*.

KEY POINTS

- Control *uke*'s wrist so *uke*'s thumb points away from you.
- Control *uke*'s shoulder with your hand across the throat or by grabbing the lapel.
- Thrust your hips directly into the extended elbow joint while pulling *uke*'s wrist and head back.

Ude hishigi ashi gatame

(leg arm lock)

Ashi gatame is performed when you are beside *uke*, who is either face down on the ground or face up. A straight arm lock using your leg or foot is called *ashi gatame*, so there are many variations.

KEY POINTS

- Apply *kesa gatame*.
- If *uke* frees the arm, grab the wrist to straighten the arm and place the elbow over your thigh.
- Apply downward pressure on the wrist with your foot, knee and/or hand.

Ude hishigi te gatame

(hand arm lock)

As the name implies, *te gatame* uses only your hands to extend the arm and put pressure on the elbow.

KEY POINTS
- Immediately after throwing *uke,* control the wrist with one hand.
- With the other hand reach under *uke*'s arm and across *uke*'s throat to grip the far lapel, fingers inside, anchoring it and preventing *uke* from turning.
- Draw *uke*'s arm across your own arm as you straighten your own arm into the elbow.

Ude hishigi sankaku gatame

(triangle arm lock)

This is very similar to the position of the choking technique, *sankaku jime,* except in this case you use the trapped arm to apply an arm bar. Like the choke, it can be applied from many different positions.

KEY POINTS
- Trap *uke*'s head and one arm between your legs.
- Lock your legs together with one foot behind your other knee to form the triangle.
- Pull *uke*'s wrist to your chest to straighten the arm as you thrust your hips into *uke*'s elbow.

APPLICATION FROM THE BOTTOM POSITION

Ashi garami

(entangled leg lock)

This immobilization and knee lock is included in the forms of grappling (*Katame no Kata*) as an example of a transition from a throwing technique to a grappling technique on the ground. It is also the only example in *Katame no Kata* of a joint lock that is not on the elbow. It is prohibited in competition and free practice due to safety concerns over applying joint locks to the knees. It must be practiced with care and control.

Ashi garami can be practiced as a follow-up attack to a failed *tomoe nage*. When *tomoe nage* is attempted and you fail to achieve good *kuzushi*, you may find yourself on your back between the legs of a standing *uke*. Use your right foot to push his left leg out, pull *uke* forward, and wrap your left leg over and around your opponent's right leg. As *uke* falls to his front, slide your left foot into *uke*'s abdomen to lock it in place. Straighten your leg to apply pressure against the side of *uke*'s knee for the submission.

KEY POINTS

- Slide deep between *uke*'s legs in a *tomoe nage* position.
- Pull *uke* forward and down as you use your right foot to push his left leg out so *uke* falls face down to your right side.
- Tuck your left foot under *uke*'s abdomen so his own weight traps his right leg to immobilize him.

NEXT STEPS TOWARDS MASTERY

When you have learned everything required to advance from white belt to black belt it is easy to think you have mastered judo. Many of your friends and acquaintances will reinforce this idea; it's part of popular culture. You have earned respect, but judo always gives us a dose of reality. Like most things worthwhile, mastery seems to grow nearer, yet remain beyond our reach.

Mastery of the gentle way takes more effort than most people want to give. Judo is complicated; skill is hard to acquire. Expertise in just one facet of judo doesn't make a master. Developing your body, mind and spirit comes along the path, but never ends. Winning tournaments, teaching successful students, or practice for 50 years may still not make you feel like a master of judo, even though others might consider you to be one.

Some accomplishments are so huge that you can't help but feel like you've arrived at mastery: winning a World Championship, successfully coaching a national team at the Olympic Games, achieving a 10th dan for your life's work. Such success is exceedingly rare and special. Yet even those who have earned our utmost respect find new doors to open and goals to achieve.

Of course, it is perfectly legitimate to retire from judo when you're unable to participate due to age or health. If you have no desire to practice judo, you are not compelled to continue. After earning a gold medal, one might feel they have reached the pinnacle. Mastery of all aspects of judo is not necessary to be highly successful. It isn't even really a thing to try for any more than achieving tenth degree black belt. But if you love it and want to continue, there is much to be done.

So when are you approaching a high level? Maybe when your judo friends are more like family, or when you have touched the lives of more students than those you have actually practiced with. Maybe when you have awarded more black belt degrees than your age, or when you have worn out more *judogi* than shoes. It could also be when thoughts of others exceed thoughts of yourself.

You will never "know" judo and then be able to quit. In reality, it's a lifelong process, more a path to follow than a destination. To master judo, seek an elusive perfection of character the rest of your life, and make a positive impact on society. Think of it, though, as master yourself.

"What judo does, is try to find the best you."

– Hayward Nishioka, 9th dan

KEEP ADVANCING

What would it take to achieve mastery of judo? A lifetime of seeking technical excellence and ever-greater accomplishments. To master judo you have to show high level competitive success and be an expert in all aspects of judo – *randori*, *kata*, *newaza*, self-defense, combat theory, principles, history, etc. Furthermore, you would have to refine your character, give back to judo, and ultimately contribute something valuable to society. We have some wonderful examples in our midst, but even the greatest judoka admit it is always a work in progress. The key? Keep advancing.. Always move forward. Don't give up on your quest for mastery.

Recognize your strengths, but confront your weaknesses. In judo we fight for a decisive victory. Do the same with your doubts, fears, lethargy, and any other obstacle. The principles of judo will guide you through the way of flexibility. When you hit a wall, go around it.

The judo rank system provides one way to gauge success, but pursuing higher rank is not the ultimate goal. You must acquire the habit of challenging, dedicating, developing, and perfecting yourself. This habit can help carry you through tough times. Just be honest with yourself and don't think you know everything. No one rightly calls themselves a judo grandmaster.

The pursuit of knowledge is an important virtue in judo practice. Yet, the more you know, the more you realize one's ignorance. Each revelation or achievement in your study reveals more areas of inquiry. If you are looking, it is not hard to find ways to advance. Do it long enough and you can achieve your highest potential. Maximizing your potential is what success is all about.

Success is achievable, but it is not simply "found" at the end of the road, it is earned all along the path.

"Ride the horse in the direction it is going"

How to master judo

You can never become too proficient in the technical basis for good judo. For example, set a goal to learn every technique recognized by the Kodokan, including numerous variations, follow-ups, escapes and defenses for each. Broaden your knowledge of judo *waza* while you deepen it with intensive study and skill practice. Include the conditions necessary for success with each technique, how to apply them in different *randori* situations, how to transition smoothly between attacks or between defense and attack. Discover how to use your knowledge to win in *shiai*. Learn to teach the techniques successfully. Finally, help your students become the best version of themselves.

Here are three important steps to higher level advancement in judo:

COMPETING

Success in competition is an irrefutable measure of your level of mastery. Some would say it is the only measure.

There is no question that a World Champion or Olympic Gold Medalist has proven their excellence. A champion who has defeated all challengers from around the world must be able to control every opponent. Winners aren't superior just on tournament day, they also know everything about the preparation and training needed for technical skill and ultimate success. Like high-performance athletes in any sport, they are experts. Those who rise to the top tier in judo deserve our respect and support. They speak with authority and know what makes judo work.

The road to mastery begins with competition, and a high level of competitive success is a requirement to be considered a master. Competition is the best way to hone your skills so they work reliably against opponents equally skilled and motivated to win. Along the way you will have to focus your determination to overcome every obstacle without any thought of giving up. Through austere practice and the challenges of competition, judo aims

If you win, do not boast of your victory; if you lose, do not be discouraged. When it is safe, do not be careless; when it is dangerous, do not fear. Simply continue down the path ahead.
– Jigoro Kano

to cultivate a strong and flexible state of mind. Furthermore, you will develop the fighting spirit from which great champions are forged.

It is never too late for advanced students to join in and discover the secrets that can only be revealed in combat. If you don't become a champion, you will inevitably get better. After all, we usually learn more from our losses than our wins.

KATA/TECHNICAL KNOWLEDGE

Kata practice is the traditional way to achieve technical mastery, adapted from the practice of jujutsu. As such, it's a connection to the roots of judo. Kodokan *kata* provides the opportunity to practice self-defense techniques, both modern and ancient. This includes striking, wrist locks, use of weapons, and other techniques not allowed in *randori*. Judo is considered a close combat martial art, but *kata* expands your study to include other combat distances. The study of *kata* also will reveal much about the appropriate mindset for attack and defense.

The *Nage no Kata* and *Katame no Kata* are focused on throwing and grappling techniques utilized in judo free practice. They build greater proficiency by studying how to use *randori* techniques to defend against strikes and other forms of aggression. These are the primary forms of *kata* learned by judo students through the first few ranks of black belt. The more advanced *kata* are an opportunity to learn the art of attack and defense in broader terms. Many people enjoy learning diverse *kata* that focus on weapon defense, judo combat theory, or principles of gentleness (*ju*).

The meaning of *kata* eludes all but the most experienced and technically proficient practitioners of judo, but expertise in all the Kodokan techniques and *kata* is a requirement for advancement towards higher grades of black belt and proficiency in judo.

Kata competition takes place at most tournaments from local events to World Championships where participants of all ages and ranks try to hone their technical skills.

TEACHING/COACHING/LEADING

A characteristic of a master is their leadership in teaching, developing, and promoting judo around the world. Such leadership is required to earn high ranks in judo. There are many ways to contribute to judo, but the first is teaching.

In order to teach judo you need considerable experience, but also a willingness to re-examine

I took what I was given and made it better. What I made better I then improved. What I improved I now strive to perfect.

your understanding of techniques so that you can explain and demonstrate the principles that make them work, the variations used in different situations, the adaptations needed for specific students, and, of course, the best ways to train for success. Teaching requires proficiency in a wide variety of training methods, but also excellent communication and motivational skills. Coaching athletes for competive success requires further study, such as development of individualized training plans incorporating tactics, strategy, fitness, etc.

The more you push yourself in judo, for example by fighting tougher opponents, the more you will start to see benefits like self-confidence. Confidence is built on accomplishment. It comes from being fearless and achieving things you never thought possible. It is connected to bravery, but requires constant self-assessment, planning, goals, and follow through. It takes years of hard work to be sure your confidence is based on an accurate examination of your character and ability.

The confidence you gain from judo helps in the development of leadership skills. Leadership and sports are linked, judo is no exception. After achieving the black belt rank, you will have gained tremendous knowledge enabling you to lead others seeking their own ascension to higher levels. Becoming a *sensei* is one of the most rewarding and challenging accomplishments in judo. Make sure you leave something of yourself for future generations of *judoka*.

The goal of judo is greater than just improving yourself. It extends to improving society. This requires leadership, and an understanding of how to use judo principles in the larger world.

FOR THE REST OF US

An outward sign of mastery in judo is the rare tenth degree black belt (*judan*). High ranks recognize extraordinary accomplishments and *judan* are the cream of the crop. By definition, few people can be considered a master of judo, and there have been very few *judan*. As we get older it becomes more difficult to think of being the best in the world or even practicing at the same pace, but there may be greater things yet ahead.

Expertise comes from deliberate practice of skills you don't do well (or at all). This is how you grow. Your commitment must be considerable, specific, and sustained to reach mastery in each aspect of judo, from *newaza* to *tachiwaza*, and *kata* to *shiai*. Only someone with a habit of making that commitment can potentially master judo over a lifetime.

But the satisfaction of learning judo does not stop when you are a black belt, so make the commitment, even when it gets more difficult. Put the same effort into training and studying for each black belt promotion as you did the first. Fortunately, your *sensei* and other role models can inspire you to seek higher levels, just don't expect it to be easy or quick.

Challenge yourself by creating new technique variations, drills, games, lessons, demonstrations, posters, studies, etc. Use your knowledge and creativity to put the art back in martial arts. Keep judo alive, share the lessons you learn from judo, support the judo community, stay involved, and make an impact (*Ippon*).

MASTER THE BASICS

When in doubt, always return to this principle. Strengthen your basic skills for the remedy when you reach a plateau or stall in your training. You simply cannot succeed for long in *randori*, *shiai*, *kata*, or teaching without maintaining competency in the basics. The judo path begins

Judo teaches us training. You have to train, but you have to be spontaneous. If you start being spontaneous without training, your bad habits will get worse and worse... Now the purpose of Judo technique is to show you this and enable you to master what has been learnt in the past - and then to become spontaneous and free. You have to train and then you have to jump beyond the training.

– Trevor Leggett, The Dragon Mask

with technical proficiency, but the good news is that a solid foundation will last a lifetime.

Especially given a finite amount of training time, your efforts will be rewarded by honing your favorite techniques until they become fearsome weapons that others can't prevent, even if they know you're about to attack. The basic techniques must be sharpened so you can apply them without thinking about it. Then you can act on fleeting opportunities.

Although specializing in a few techniques is powerful, developing a variety of attacks broadens your response to a wider range of opportunities. As you advance, you should find it easier to apply techniques that were previously too difficult, so continue to revisit them. *Judoka* who master the basics can freely modify a technique to fit the situation and capitalize on any tiny crack in an opponent's defense. Develop your own methods that build on your strengths to empower you to freely attack in unique ways.

Combination techniques are a basic skill and *yudansha* are expected to be proficient in them. Whether you are trying to improve your tournament results, perform better in *randori*, or understand combat theory, moving fluidly between attacks is vital. As an example of basic skills applied in more advanced ways, think about how to train for *renzoku waza* (continuous combination of techniques) and *renraku henka* (connection and change).

Renzoku waza are combination techniques that are tied together and performed in succession without letting *uke* regain balance. Each attack is followed by the same technique (with any necessary adjustments) or another technique in the same direction. Each attack takes advantage of the *kuzushi* from the previous technique as you relentlessly pursue the *ippon*. The result is that not only do you seize the initiative, you keep it.

The Kodokan defines *renraku henka* as follows:

> *For both attacking and defending, as one of the most important aspects of applying techniques effectively it is considered essential to be able to create good connection between continuously applied techniques so that each evolves into the next. This can include both changing a technique of your own into another technique of your own, or changing your opponent's technique into a technique of your own. In either case it is necessary to cultivate your ability to move logically and efficiently from one technique into another.*

This can only be achieved after mastering the basics and considerable *randori*, but it is the epitome of judo and breathtaking to see. Well trained opponents will not make obvious mistakes, so take advantage of small lapses in focus or balance. Every attack causes a defensive move which creates a predictable opportunity to attack again. By anticipating these opportunities, you can develop the flexibility to transition from one technique to another without a gap. The attacks must be natural and fit with the circumstances, especially your opponent's reaction to the previous attack. Your objective should be to build a web that your opponent cannot escape from.

Drills can help you integrate attacks into a sequence that gives *uke* little opportunity to recover, but do not expect to perform the entire drill sequence in *randori*. Use drills to develop your ability to recognize *uke*'s defense and move fluidly from a technique to another while keeping your opponent off balance. The sequence cannot be pre-determined since *uke*'s reaction may vary, so drill to develop the ability to combine attacks spontaneously.

Start with a familiar series that pushes *uke* back until he resists and is vulnerable in the opposite direction:

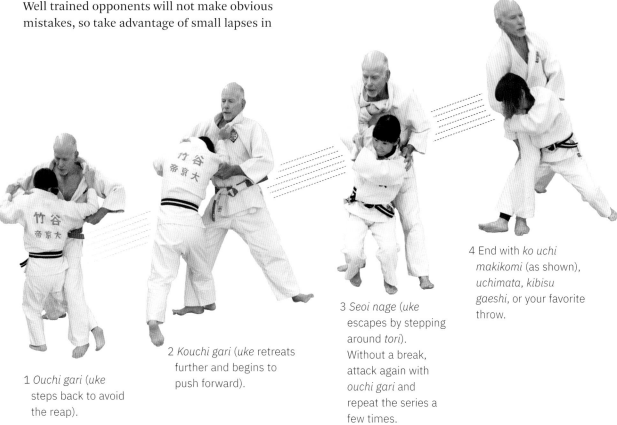

1 *Ouchi gari* (*uke* steps back to avoid the reap).

2 *Kouchi gari* (*uke* retreats further and begins to push forward).

3 *Seoi nage* (*uke* escapes by stepping around *tori*). Without a break, attack again with *ouchi gari* and repeat the series a few times.

4 End with *ko uchi makikomi* (as shown), *uchimata, kibisu gaeshi,* or your favorite throw.

Each attack must be realistic, so practice completing throws if *uke* does not escape. Begin by throwing *uke* with the first throw. Repeat the same technique, but now *uke* is prepared and escapes, so you throw with the second technique. Repeat the sequence again. When *uke* escapes both attacks, then throw with the third technique. Repeat for each subsequent throw then start over.

Begin practicing in cooperative *kata* style with little resistance and agreed-upon escapes from *uke*. Once you have learned the sequence, *uke* should vary escapes so you learn to react in real time. Eventually allow *uke* to freely respond with escapes, blocks, or counter attacks while you pursue a successful throw. Substitute your favorite techniques to practice your own combinations.

Of course, the same kind of drill can be applied to *kaeshi waza*, *newaza*, and the often overlooked transition from *tachi waza* to *newaza*. When you finish any throwing technique, do not stop or relax but move quickly into a pin or submission. As pointed out in "Judo Formal Techniques" by Otaki and Draeger, "This example borders on the advanced study of connection-variation techniques (*renraku henka waza),* and it is based on *zanshin*." Finish every attack with the state of awareness and readiness that permits you to see the next action. Never neglect your mental preparation.

Example drills:

a. *Kouchi gari* (*uke*'s foot escapes by stepping back), *ouchi gari* (*uke* pushes forward), uchimata (*uke* steps around), repeat immediately

b. *Tomoe nage* to guard, *juji gatame, uki gatame, ude garami* (to break grip), *juji gatame*

Tomoe nage

Juji gatame

Ude garami

Uki gatame

c. *Kosoto gari, osoto gari, harai goshi, kuzure kesa gatame*

d. *Deashi harai, harai goshi, osotogari, osoto makikomi, ura gatame*

e. *Sasae tsurikomi ashi, okuriashi harai, taiotoshi, juji gatame*

f. Using a left-sided grip, attack to the right side (see below) with hopping *osoto gari*, *tai otoshi*, *kouchi gari*, *ouchi gari*, *uchi mata*, then continue in *newaza*.

Osoto gari

tai otoshi

kouchi gari

uchi mata

ouchi gari

FINAL SUGGESTIONS TO ADVANCE IN JUDO

1. Cross train

Cross training is the commonly accepted sports practice of supplementing your sport specific training with related training that builds on your strengths, or improves your weaker areas. Simple examples are to lift weights to gain strength or run to improve endurance. For skill training, many judo students practice BJJ, wrestling, jujutsu or other martial arts to work intensively on special areas such as submissions, self-defense, or no-gi grappling.

"If someone asked me what a human being ought to devote the maximum of his time to, I would answer, 'Training.' Train more than you sleep."

– Masutatsu Oyama

2. Referee

Referees have the best seat in the house. If you want to learn from competition successes and failures, there is a lot to be said for refereeing. Not only do you gain from seeing top competitors in action, but the training helps you more clearly understand the objectives and tactics on the mat. To officiate correctly you have to understand modern judo techniques and study constantly to keep up your ability.

Refereeing also develops a strong judo state-of-mind; one that is calm and observant, yet decisive and in control. You can't let the athlete, coach, or crowd disturb your sense of balance. You must remain in the moment ready to make a critical call in an instant.

3. Seek what you need

You can expand your knowledge of judo by seeing how it is done around the world, or even around the corner. Visit places outside your *dojo* to learn more about judo. Practice at the Kodokan Judo Institute in Tokyo, or help a developing country with your expertise. Train with an Olympian, or the highest ranked instructor you can find, to improve your judo fast. Attend training camps and clinics as much as possible. Good judo is always welcoming and accessible.

4. Serve

At some point, we all shift somewhat from developing our own skills on the mat to helping others reach their goals. There are many ways to help and you will find that your contributions matter. Volunteer for positions with your national organization, become a *kata* judge, contribute research, promote judo online, support aspiring athletes, or assist at your club. Most of all, be a good example.

5. Expand your practice

Apply what you have learned in judo to the rest of your life. Study the meaning of judo through its application in business principles, de-escalation techniques, difficult relationships, bravely facing challenges, and never giving up in the face of defeat. Continue using judo, even when you can't get on the mat.

6. Share

Research, study, discover, and communicate information to motivate or educate a wide audience. Judo is such a valuable endeavor that we should all share it. Write a book, make a video, create an online resource, or give a clinic. Students need the encouragement and support that teachers can give. Oddly enough, teachers also need the support that only students can give. Both must advance, moving forward for the sake of the other. This is the way.

Once you've earned your black belt (*shodan*), you are at the beginning of a journey that could take a lifetime. The black belt path has ten ranks, each requiring significant accomplishments as you seek to master judo. You are grappling with an art that won't submit, won't always let you go home a winner. Judo is bigger than you, stronger than you, and impeccably balanced. It brings powerful lessons that make you a better person.

Much like your *sensei*, judo motivates and encourages you. You share a bond that cannot be broken. Judo gives great joy, understanding, a framework for success, and a goal. At the same

When you get thrown, you learn to prevent it from happening again by being more aware and keeping your balance. When you are pinned, you learn to take action earlier to control your own future. When you are forced to submit to pain, you become more determined to make changes. When you are choked, you vow to take the initiative before life takes you down. When you are defeated, you learn to never leave your destiny to others. Judo requires that you move beyond whatever is blocking your progress. It insists you grasp the larger lessons it offers.

A black belt rank means you are well-prepared to take another step forward. Each achievement makes the next challenge easier. Judo provides everything you need to overcome any obstacle, but you must provide the effort. Mastering judo is a worthy contest. Just don't tap out.

APPENDICES

APPENDIX 1:
Techniques recognized by the Kodokan

Deashi harai (1st group)

| Deashi harai | Hiza guruma | Sasae tsurikomi ashi | Uki goshi | Osoto gari | O goshi | Ouchi gari | Seoi nage |

Dai Nikyo (2nd group)

| Kosoto gari | Kouchi gari | Koshi guruma | Tsurikomi goshi | Okuri ashi harai | Tai otoshi | Harai goshi | Uchi mata |

Sankyo (3rd group)

| Kosoto gake | Tsuri goshi | Yoko otoshi | Ashi guruma | Hane goshi | Harai tsurikomi ashi | Tomoe nage | Kata guruma |

Yonkyo (4th group)

| Sumi gaeshi | Tani otoshi | Hane makikomi | Sukui nage | Utsuri goshi | O guruma | Soto makikomi | Uki otoshi |

Gokyo (5th group)

| Osoto guruma | Uki waza | Yoko wakare | Yoko guruma | Ushiro goshi | Ura nage | Sumi otoshi | Yoko gake |

Habukareta Waza
(techniques from 1895 gokyo no waza)
Obi otoshi
Seoi otoshi
Yama arashi
Osoto otoshi
Daki wakare
Hikikomi gaeshi
Tawara gaeshi
Uchi makikomi

Shinmeisho no waza
(newly accepted techniques)
Morote gari
Kibisu gaeshi
Kouchi gaeshi
Osoto gaeshi
Uchi mata gaeshi
Kani basami
Kawazu gake

Uchi mata makikomi
Ippon seoi nage
Kuchiki taoshi
Uchi mata sukashi
Tsubame gaeshi
Ouchi gaeshi
Harai goshi gaeshi

Hane goshi gaeshi
Osoto maki komi
Harai maki komi
Sode tsurikomi goshi
Obi tori gaeshi
Kouchi makikomi

The 32 *newaza* techniques recognized by the Kodokan Judo Institute

Osaekomi waza
Kesa gatame
Kuzure kesa gatame
Ushiro kesa gatame
Kata gatame
Kami shiho gatame
Kuzure kami shiho gatame
Yoko shiho gatame
Tate shiho gatame
Uki gatame
Ura gatame

Shime waza
Nami juji jime
Gyaku juji jime
Kata juji jime
Hadaka jime
Okuri eri jime
Kataha jime
Katate jime
Ryote jime
Sode guruma jime
Tsukkomi jime
Sankaku jime
Do jime

Kansetsu waza
Ude garami
Ude hishigi juji gatame
Ude hishigi ude gatame
Ude hishigi hiza gatame
Ude hishigi waki gatame
Ude hishigi hara gatame
Ude hishigi ashi gatame
Ude hishigi sankaku gatame
Ashi garami
Ude hishigi te gatame

Forms *(kata)*

Nage no kata (Throwing forms)

Te waza (hand techniques)
• Uki otoshi
• Seoi nage
• Kata guruma

Koshi waza (hip techniques)
• Uki goshi
• Harai goshi
• Tsurikomi goshi

Ashi waza (foot/leg techniques)
• Okuri ashi harai
• Sasae tsurikomi ashi
• Uchi mata

Ma sutemi waza (rear sacrifice techniques)
• Tomoe nage
• Ura nage
• Sumi gaeshi

Yoko sutemi waza (side sacrifice techniques)
• Yoko gake
• Yoko guruma
• Uki waza

Yoko sutemi waza (side sacrifice techniques)
• Yoko gake
• Yoko guruma
• Uki waza

Katame no kata (Grappling forms)

Osaekomi waza (pinning techniques)
• Kesa gatame
• Kata gatame
• Kamishiho gatame
• Yokoshiho gatame
• Kuzure kamishiho gatame

Shime waza (choking techniques)
• Kata juji jime
• Hadaka jime
• Okuri eri jime
• Kataha jime
• Gyaku juji jime

Kansetsu waza (joint locking techniques)
• Ude garami
• Ude hishigi juji gatame
• Ude hishigi ude gatame
• Ude hishigi hiza gatame
• Ashi garami

Combination and counter techniques *(kaeshi and renraku waza)*

This table gives you an idea of how to combine various throws into effective integrated attack systems. Throwing techniques are listed in alphabetical order by the Japanese name, followed by the throws that can be used in combination to set up your opponent for the first throw, or to attack an opponent who has escaped your first attempt at a throw. The last column gives examples of what throws to use to counter an attack by your opponent.

    The appropriate follow-up technique depends largely on exactly how your opponent attempts to escape your first throw. The appropriate counter also depends on exploiting the weakness in your opponent's technique, so not every counter will work the same against different attackers. In some cases, a right-sided attack is followed by a left-sided combination or counter. While this list is comprehensive, many other *kaeshi waza* and *renraku waza* can be used to throw your opponent.

THROWING TECHNIQUE	SET-UP ATTACK	FOLLOW-UP ATTACK	COUNTERATTACK
Ashi guruma Foot wheel	Deashi harai Okuriashi harai Osoto gari	Osoto gari Tai otoshi	Nidan kosoto gari Te guruma Sukui nage
Deashi harai Advancing foot sweep	Ouchi gari	Tai otoshi Morote seoi nage	Tsubame gaeshi Harai goshi
Hane goshi Spring hip throw	Deashi harai Okuriashi harai Kouchi gari	Ouchi gari Kouchi gari Hane makikomi	Hane goshi gaeshi Ushiro goshi Utsuri goshi Tani otoshi Yoko guruma
Harai goshi Sweeping hip throw	Deashi harai Kouchi gari Osoto gari	Osoto gari Harai makikomi Ashi guruma	Ushiro goshi Te guruma Utsuri goshi Ura nage Harai goshi gaeshi
Hiza guruma Knee wheel	Osoto gari Deashi harai	Osoto gari Kosoto gari Deashi harai Harai goshi	Kouchi gari Kuchiki taoshi Ouchi gari
Kani basami Flying scissors	Harai goshi O guruma	Ne waza	Tani otoshi Nidan kosoto gari
Koshi guruma Hip wheel	Ouchi gari Harai goshi	Osoto gari Ouchi gari Soto makikomi	Ushiro goshi Utsuri goshi Tani otoshi
Kosoto gake Small outside hook	Okuriashi harai Deashi harai	Kosoto gari Tai otoshi Ouchi gari	Uchi mata Ouchi gari

THROWING TECHNIQUE	SET-UP ATTACK	FOLLOW-UP ATTACK	COUNTERATTACK
Kosoto gari Small outside reap	Hiza guruma Ouchi gari Uki goshi	Sasae tsurikomi ashi Kibisu gaeshi Nidan kosoto gari Harai goshi Tai otoshi	Uchi mata Kani basami Ouchi gari
Kouchi gari Small inner reap	Ouchi gari Uchi mata Ippon seoi nage Tai otoshi	Ouchi gari Seoi nage Kuchiki taoshi Harai tsurikomi ashi	Hiza guruma Nidan kosoto gari Kouchi gaeshi Tani otoshi Tomoe nage
Kouchi makikomi Small inner wraparound	Ouchi gari Ippon seoi nage Kouchi gari	Ouchi gari Ippon seoi nage	Hiza guruma Sumi gaeshi Kouchi gaeshi
Morote gari Two hand reap	Kosoto gari Seoi nage	Kouchi makikomi Ouchi gari	Tawara gaeshi Sumi gaeshi Hikikomi gaeshi Uchi mata
Nidan kosoto gari Double outside reap	Osoto gari Kosoto gari	Tani otoshi	Uchi mata Ouchi gari
O goshi Large hip throw	Ouchi gari Kouchi gari Uki goshi	Ouchi gari Kouchi gari Harai goshi	Ushiro goshi Utsuri goshi Yoko guruma Tani otoshi
O guruma Large wheel	Deashi harai	Kani basami Ashi guruma	Ushiro goshi Utsuri goshi Tani otoshi
Okuriashi harai Sliding foot sweep	Sasae tsurikomi ashi	Tai Otoshi Harai Goshi Seoi Otoshi Seoi Nage	Tsubame Gaeshi Harai Goshi Kouchi Gari
Osoto gari Large outer reap	Harai goshi Seoi nage Ashi guruma	Nidan kosoto gari Sasae tsurikomi ashi Harai goshi Hiza guruma Osoto makikomi Osoto otoshi Uchi mata	Osoto gaeshi Harai goshi Osoto makikomi Ura nage Sukui nage
Ouchi gari Large inner reap	Kouchi gari Tai otoshi Tsuri goshi Hane goshi Osoto gari	Uchi mata Tai otoshi Osoto gari Kouchi gari	Ouchi gaeshi Nidan kosoto gari Ippon seoi nage Tomoe nage

THROWING TECHNIQUE	SET-UP ATTACK	FOLLOW-UP ATTACK	COUNTERATTACK
Sasae tsurikomi ashi Propping lifting pulling throw	Osoto gari	Harai goshi Osoto gari	Kouchi gari Ouchi gari Osoto gari
Seoi nage Shoulder throw	Kouchi gari Osoto gari	Kouchi gari Osoto gari Sukui nage Uchi makikomi Seoi otoshi	Ushiro goshi Sukui nage Utsuri goshi Tani otoshi Okuri eri jime
Seoi otoshi Shoulder drop	Deashi harai Ouchi gari	Ouchi gari Osoto gari Kibisu gaeshi	Kosoto gake Okuri eri jime
Sode tsurikomi goshi Sleeve lifting pulling hip	Ouchi gari Osoto gari	Ouchi gari Osoto gari	Ushiro goshi Sukui nage Tani otoshi
Sumi gaeshi Corner reversal	Deashi harai Ouchi gari	Ouchi gari Juji gatame	Ouchi gari Kuchiki taoshi
Tai otoshi Body drop	Deashi harai Ouchi gari Tai otoshi	Tai otoshi Ouchi gari Yoko tomoe nage Kouchi gari	Kosoto gake Yoko guruma
Tani otoshi Valley drop	Kosoto gari Harai goshi	Nidan kosoto gari	Uchi mata Ouchi gari
Tomoe nage Circular throw	Deashi harai Tai otoshi	Juji gatame	Ouchi gari Kouchi gari Kuchiki taoshi
Tsuri goshi Lifting hip	Kouchi gari Ouchi gari	Kouchi gari Ouchi gari Harai goshi	Ushiro goshi Sukui nage Utsuri goshi O goshi Tani otoshi Ura nage
Tsurikomi goshi Lifting pulling hip	Kouchi gari Ouchi gari	Kouchi gari Ouchi gari	Ushiro goshi Sukui nage Utsuri goshi Tani otoshi
Uchi mata Inner thigh throw	Kouchi gari Ouchi gari Deashi harai Osoto gari	Tai otoshi Kouchi gari Ouchi gari Uchi mata makikomi	Uchi mata gaeshi Uchi mata sukashi Te guruma Ura nage

Tournament rules and scoring

START OF A CONTEST
After the contestants have entered the competition area, they bow to each other and take one step forward, then the referee announces *hajime* (begin) to start the contest.

Scoring a contest
- *Ippon* (full point)
- *Waza ari* (almost *ippon* or half point)

Penalties
- *Hansoku make* (very serious violation; disqualification)
- Shido (minor violation; warning. After three shido the contestant will be disqualified.)

OBJECTIVE
In judo competition the objective is to score an *ippon*. Once it is obtained the competition ends. A match can be won by any of the following methods:

- Skillful execution of a recognized judo throwing technique that results in a contestant being thrown. The four criteria that must be present for *ippon* are speed, force, landing on the back, and control until the end of the landing. If *uke* avoids landing on his back by landing in a bridge on his head, it will also be considered *ippon* to discourage a dangerous situation.

- Maintaining control of an opponent in a pin for 20 seconds.
- One contestant cannot continue and submits to a pin, choke, or armlock by tapping twice.
- One contestant is disqualified for violating the rules (*hansoku make*).
- Applying an effective choke that results in unconsciousness.
- Earning two *waza ari* (near *ippon*). A *waza ari* can be earned by: (1) a throwing technique that is not quite an *ippon* (e.g. the opponent lands only partly on the back, or with less force than required for *ippon*); or (2) holding a contestant in a pin for at least 10 seconds. *Waza ari* criteria for a throw that is not fully on the back is (1) a landing on the whole side of the body at 90 degrees or more to the rear, or (2) on one shoulder and upper back, or (3) on both elbows or hands or one elbow and one hand, towards the back.

In the event of a tied score at the end of the match time, a Golden Score period begins and contestants continue to fight. The first one to earn a score wins.

Modifications are made for children and novice divisions at local tournaments where, for example, chokes and armlocks are not permitted.

Ippon (full point):
Opponent is thrown on the back with force and speed, held under control in a pin on the mat for 20 seconds, or an effective choke or arm lock is applied.

Waza ari (near ippon):
Throw is not completely successful, or opponent is held under control in a pin for at least 10 seconds.

Osaekomi
(mat hold begins):
Opponent is held under control on his or her back and the time starts.

Mate (stop):
The match is temporarily stopped and the time clock pauses.

Competition penalties and prohibited acts

Prohibited acts are divided into slight infringements that result in a warning (*shido*) and grave infringements that result in disqualification (*hansoku make*). A third *shido* automatically results in disqualification (*hansoku make*). A *hansoku make* means the contest ends, the contestant is disqualified, and may be excluded from the tournament depending on the seriousness of the infringement.

The prohibited acts in the International Judo Federation Competition Rules are used beginning 2022 for the 2024 Olympic cycle. The rules are not static and may change or be re-interpreted. In addition, national federations and tournament organizers may modify the rules for local competitions, to accommodate different age and experience levels, or for other reasons. Referees are authorized to award penalties according to the 'intent' or situation and in the best interest of the sport.

Shido (slight infringements)

1. Negative positions, against the fighting spirit, will be penalized by *shido* (to adopt in a standing position, after *kumikata*, an excessively defensive posture, not searching for an attack, a defensive attitude etc.).

2. To make an action designed to give the impression of an attack but which clearly shows that there was no intent to throw the opponent (false attack). False attacks are defined as:
   • *Tori* has no intention of throwing.
   • *Tori* attacks without *kumikata* (grip) or immediately releases the *kumikata*.
   • *Tori* makes a single fake attack or a number of repeated fake attacks with no breaking of *uke*'s balance.
   • *Tori* puts a leg in between *uke*'s legs to block the possibility of an attack.

3. Unless in accordance with Article 10, to pull the opponent down in order to start *newaza* and the latter does not take advantage of this to continue into *newaza*, the referee shall announce mate and give shido to the contestant who has infringed Article 10.

4. In a standing position, after the referee announced *Hajime* and before or after *kumikata* has been established, not to make any attacking moves. Recognizing the difficulty of preparing a throwing action, the time between *kumikata* and making an attack is extended to 45 seconds as long as there is a positive progression. The referees should penalize strictly the contestant who does not engage in *kumikata* or who tries not to be gripped by the opponent.

5. Without there being an attack engaged in a valid position (see Article 5 - Exceptions):
   In *tachi-waza* to go intentionally or intentionally force the opponent to go outside the contest area; In *ne-waza* to go deliberately outside the contest area. If an athlete puts one foot outside of the contest area without immediate attack or not returning immediately inside the contest area, he is penalized by *shido*. Two feet outside the contest area is penalized immediately by *shido*.

6. To put a hand, arm, foot or leg directly on the opponent's face. The face means the area within the line bordered by the forehead, the front of the ears and the jaw-line.

7. To intentionally avoid taking *kumikata* to prevent action in the contest. Normal *kumikata* is taking hold the right side of the opponent's *judogi*, be it the sleeve, collar, chest area, top of the shoulder or back with the left hand and with the right hand the left side of the opponent's *judogi* be it the sleeve, collar, chest area, top of the shoulder, or back and always above the belt or vice versa. To offer more chances to throw and more attractive judo, non-classical grips are allowed. Collar and lapel, one side, cross grip, belt grip, pocket and pistol grips are allowed when the attitude of the *judoka* is positive, when they are looking to perform positive attacks and throws. If taken, time will be allowed for the preparation of an attack. The same grip (or a collar and lapel grip) used to force the opponent with either one or both arms, to take a bending position, used in a defensive, negative, or blocking attitude, will be penalized by *shido*.

8. To grab below the belt.
   Exception: Gripping under the belt in the end phase of a throwing technique is allowed if the opponent is already in *ne-waza*. If the throwing

technique is interrupted, gripping under the belt is a *newaza* action.

9. Ducking beneath the opponent's arm without an immediate attack will be penalized with *shido*.

10. Hooking one leg between the opponent's legs unless immediately attacking with a throwing technique.

11. In a standing position, to continually hold the opponent's sleeve end(s) for a defensive purpose or to grasp by "screwing up" the sleeve end(s).

12. In a standing position, to continually keep the opponent's fingers of one or both hands interlocked, to prevent action in the contest or to take the wrist or the hands of the opponent only to avoid the grip or the attack on him.

13. To insert a finger or fingers inside the opponent's sleeve or of his trousers either in the ends of the trouser legs or in the waistband (top) of the trousers.

14. To bend back the opponent's finger(s) in order to break his or her grip.

15. Breaking the grips with one or two hands and immediately taking grips is allowed. Breaking grips with one or two hands and not taking a grip immediately is *shido*.

16. To break the grip of the opponent with the knee or leg.

17. Cover the upper part of the lapel of the *judogi* jacket to prevent the grip.

18. Avoid *uke*'s grip with a blow on his arm or hand.

19. Blocking the opponent's hand.

20. Leg grabbing, grabbing the trousers, blocking, or pushing the opponent's leg(s) with their hands or arms. It is possible to grip the leg only when the two opponents are in a clear *ne-waza* position and the *tachi-waza* action has stopped.

21. To encircle the end of the belt or jacket around any part of the opponent's body. The act of "encircling" means that the belt or jacket must completely encircle. Using the belt or jacket as an anchor for a grip (without encircling), e.g. to trap the opponent's arm, should not be penalized.

22. To take the *judogi* in the mouth (either his or her own or the opponent's *judogi*).

23. To put a foot or a leg in the opponent's belt, collar or lapel.

24. To apply *shime-waza* using either your own or your opponent's belt or bottom of the jacket or using only the fingers.

25. In *shime-waza* or *kansetsu-waza* over-stretching the leg is forbidden and the referee will announce *mate* immediately and sanction the athlete with *shido*.

26. To hug directly the opponent for a throw (bear hug). To attack with a bear hug the athlete must have a minimum of one grip before making the attack. It is not valid to grip simultaneously or to make a second grip consecutively. Only touching the *judogi* or the opponent's hands, is not considered as *kumikata*, gripping is necessary.

27. To apply leg scissors to the opponent's trunk (*dojime*), neck or head (scissor with crossed feet), while stretching out the legs. In *shime-waza* (e.g. *ryote-jime*) it is forbidden to use the legs crossed to assist the grip.

28. To kick with the knee or foot, the hand or arm of the opponent, in order to make him release his or her grip or to kick the opponent's leg or ankle without applying any technique.

29. If both athletes are in a *tachi-shisei* (standing position) and one or both apply *kansetsu-waza* (including *ude gaeshi* and similar) or *shime-waza* (both technical situations alone or combined with a judo throwing technique), Mate and *shido* should be announced. However, if the action is dangerous or can injure the opponent, it will be *hansoku-make*.

30. The act of entangling the leg without making an immediate attack.

31. No score and *shido* for reverse *seoi-nage*. The application of seoi-nage techniques when *uke* can perform *ukemi* and *tori* can control is allowed. In the variation of *seoi-nage* techniques when tori turns away from *uke*, twisting their *tsurite* and *hikite* using the same lapel of *uke*'s *judogi*, without controlling *uke*, standing or dropping down in an unknown direction, without giving the possibility to the opponent to perform *ukemi* and sometimes with *uke* falling with the neck on the mat, is forbidden.

32. The correct preparation of the *judogi* and belt is the responsibility of the athlete and fixing is allowed once per *judoka* per contest. Further occasions are penalized with shido. Please note that the belt cannot be untied without the permission of the referee.

   Athletes must enter and leave the field of

play wearing their *judogi* in the proper way. If the *judogi* and/or belt becomes undone during the contest the athlete is obliged to quickly fix it back to the correct position. This can be between *Mate* and *Hajime* or during any break in action. The referee will award a penalty (*shido* or hansoku-make if it is the third penalties) towards the athlete(s) who does not re-adjust their *judogi* correctly between the *mate* and the subsequent Hajime!.

To intentionally disarrange his own or his opponent's *judogi*; to untie or retie the belt or the trousers without the referee's permission; to intentionally lose time arranging his *judogi* and belt.

33. Retying hair is allowed once per judoka per contest. Further occasions are penalized with shido. The correct preparation of arranging hair is essential and is the responsibility of each athlete.

Hansoku make (grave infringements)

FOR DANGEROUS TECHNIQUES:

1. To "dive" headfirst, onto the *tatami* by bending forward and downward while performing or attempting to perform techniques such as *uchi-mata*, *harai-goshi*, *kata-guruma*, etc. it is forbidden to somersault forward when *uke* is on the shoulders or the back of *tori*.

2. Head defense, to ensure that judo has as little trauma as possible, if *uke* attempts voluntarily to use the head with any movement which is dangerous for the head, neck or spine, for defense and to avoid landing in/escaping from a score he shall be penalized with *hansoku-make*.

FOR ACTS AGAINST THE SPIRIT OF JUDO:

1. To apply *kawazu-gake* (to throw the opponent by winding one leg around the opponent's leg, while facing more or less in the same direction as the opponent and falling backwards into him). Even if the thrower twists/turns during the throwing action, this should still be considered "*kawazu-gake*" and be penalized. Techniques such as *o-soto-gari*, *o-uchi-gari*, and *uchi-mata* where the foot/leg is entwined with opponent's leg will be permitted and should be scored.

2. The application of *kani-basami* (scissors throw) and *do-jime* (applying leg scissors to the opponent's trunk, neck, or head while stretching out the legs with crossed feet).

3. To apply *kansetsu-waza* anywhere other than to the elbow joint.

4. To fall directly to the *tatami* while applying or attempting to apply techniques such as *ude-hishigi-waki-gatame*.

5. Applying *kansetsu-waza* or *shime-waza* in *tachi-shisei* with a judo throwing technique will be penalized with *hansoku-make*.

6. *Uke*, when behind *tori*, cannot reap *tori*'s leg or legs from the inside.

7. To make any action that may endanger or injure the opponent especially the opponent's neck or spinal vertebrae.

8. To intentionally fall backwards when the other contestant is clinging to his or her back and when either athlete has control of the other's movement.

9. To lift the opponent off the *tatami* and forcefully push him back onto the *tatami* without a judo technique.

10. To disregard the referee's instructions.

11. To make unnecessary calls, remarks or gestures derogatory to the opponent or referee during the contest.

12. To wear or to have inside the *judogi* a hard or metallic object (covered or not).

13. Any action against the spirit of judo (this includes anything that can be described as anti-judo, for example being in the lead and in the last seconds of the match leaving the competition area to prevent the opponent from taking grips) may be punished by a direct *hansoku-make* at any time in the contest.

Online resources

These web sites are considered to be the most
reliable sources of information about judo.

IJF.org
The International Judo Federation has details on
international competition, including contest rules
and contacts for national judo organizations in
each country.

kodokanjudoinstitute.org
The Kodokan Judo Institute in Tokyo, Japan is the
original school of judo founded by Jigoro Kano.

JudoInside.com
Top coverage of worldwide judo competition.

JudoInfo.com
Comprehensive source of information about all
aspects of judo, including online lessons, articles,
techniques, and humor.

Glossary

Aiyotsu	Same grip used by both persons, either right or left
Ashi	Foot, leg
Ashi waza	Foot/leg techniques
Atemi waza	Striking techniques
Ayumi ashi	Ordinary pattern of walking with alternating feet in front
Batsugun	Instant promotion
Budo	Martial arts (the way of war)
Bushido	Way of the warrior
Dan	Black belt rank
Debana	Instant of opportunity to break balance as opponent initiates a motion
Dojo	School or training hall for studying the way
Eri	Collar, lapel
Fudoshin	Immovable spirit
Fusegi	Escapes
Fusen gachi	Win by default
Go no sen	Reactive initiative; attacking in response to an attack
Goshin jutsu waza	Self-defense techniques
Hajime	Begin
Hando no kuzushi	Unbalancing by reaction
Hansokumake	Most serious penalty, *disqualification*
Happo no kuzushi	Breaking balance in eight directions
Hidari	Left
Hiji	Elbow
Hiki wake	No decision; tie or draw
Hikidashi	Pulling out
Hikite	Pulling hand, usually the hand gripping a sleeve
Hiza	Knee
Ippon	One point in competition
Jigotai	Defensive posture
Jime	Strangle or choke
Jita kyoei	Principle of mutual prosperity
Judo	Gentle or flexible way
Judo ichidai	Spending life in diligent pursuit of judo
Judogi	Judo practice uniform
Judoka	One who studies judo

Ju no kata	Forms of Gentleness
Ju no ri	Principle of flexibility or yielding
Jujutsu	Gentle art
Kaeshi waza	Counter techniques
Kake	Completion or execution of technique
Kansetsu waza	Joint locking techniques
Kappo (katsu)	Resuscitation techniques
Kata	Forms; also shoulder
Katame no Kata	Forms of grappling
Kenka yotsu	Opposite grips used by each person, one right/one left
Ki	Spirit, life force
Kiai	To gather spirit with a shout
Kihon	Basics, fundamentals
Kime no kata	Forms of Decision
Kinshi waza	Techniques prohibited in competition
Ki o tsuke	Attention
Kodansha	High ranking judoka, 5th dan and above
Kodokan	Judo institute in Tokyo where judo was founded
Koshi waza	Hip techniques
Kumikata	Gripping methods
Kuzure	Modified or broken hold
Kuzushi	Unbalancing the opponent
Kyu	Student rank
Maai	Space or engagement distance
Mae	Forward, front
Mae ukemi	Falling forward
Ma sutemi waza	Rear sacrifice throws
Mawarikomi	Spinning in for a throw
Mate	Stop
Migi	Right
Mizu no kokoro	Mind like water
Mudansha	Students below black belt rank
Nage	Throw
Nage no Kata	Forms of Throwing
Nagekomi	Repetitive throwing practice
Nage waza	Throwing techniques
Newaza	Techniques on the ground

Obi	Judo belt
Osaekomi	Pin, referee call to begin timing
Osaekomi waza	Pinning techniques
Osaekomi toketa	Escape, stop timing of hold
Randori	Free practice
Randori no kata	Forms of free practice techniques (*Nage no Kata* and *Katame no Kata*)
Randori waza	Techniques for free practice
Rei	Bow
Reiho	Forms of respect, manners, etiquette
Renraku waza	Combination techniques
Ritsurei	Standing bow
Seika tanden	A point in the abdomen that is the center of gravity
Seiryoku zenyo	Principle of maximum efficiency
Seiza	Formal kneeling posture
Sen	Attack initiative
Sensei	Teacher, instructor
Shiai	Contest
Shido	Penalty (minor infraction)
Shimban (shinpan)	Referee
Shime waza	Choking or strangling techniques
Shintai	Moving forward, sideways and backward
Shisei	Posture
Shizentai	Natural posture
Shomen	Front of the training hall
Sode	Sleeve
Sono mama	Stop action; referee command to freeze
Sore made	Finished, time is up
Sute geiko	*Randori* practice against a higher-level *judoka*
Sutemi waza	Sacrifice techniques
Tachi waza	Standing techniques
Tai sabaki	Body control, turning
Tatami	Mat
Te	Hand, arm
Te waza	Hand techniques
Tobikomi	Jumping in
Tokui waza	Favorite or best technique
Tori	Person performing a technique

Tsugi ashi	Walking by bringing one foot up to another
Tsukuri	Entry into a technique, positioning
Tsurite	Lifting hand
Uchikomi	Repeated practice without completion
Ude	Arm
Uke	Person receiving the technique
Ukemi	Break-fall techniques
Ushiro	Backward, rear
Ushiro sabaki	Back movement control
Ushiro ukemi	Falling backward
Waza	Technique
Waza ari	Near *ippon* or half point
Waza ari	Two *waza ari* for the win
awasete ippon	
Yakusoku renshu	Prearranged form of repetitive
(or *geiko*)	practice
Yoko	Side
Yoko sutemi waza	Side sacrifice throws
Yoko ukemi	Falling sideways
Yoshi	Resume action, referee command to continue
Yubi	Finger
Yudansha	Person who has earned black belt
Yudanshakai	Black belt association
Yusei gachi	Win by judge's decision
Zanshin	Awareness
Zarei	Kneeling bow
Zenpo kaiten ukemi	Forward rolling break-fall
Zubon	Pants

Index

Acknowledgements

The lessons shared in this book are gleaned from many years of help from teachers, training partners, students, and others. For providing the expertise seen in the high quality photos, thanks to the Encino Judo Club, Gene Demachi, Yuka Demachi, Alain Wilkinson, Mark Herrschaft, Jerrod Wilson, Justin Bennett, Alex Butcher, Ian Geustyn, Jessica Butcher, Alistair Hill, Madré Rinquest, Laura Schwormstedt and Denton Smith. Thanks to Edward Shirey for technical advice, Sean Ohlenkamp for photographic advice, and Michael Hultstrom for providing the drawings in Appendix 1. Thank you, Bernadette, for your unfailing faith and encouragement.

Photographic Credits

All photography by Ryno Reyneke and Neil Ohlenkamp, with the exception of the following photographers and/or their agencies (copyright rests with these individuals and/or their agencies).

Cover: Master1305/Shutterstock
Pages 10, 131: Dimitri Iundt/Corbis
Pages: 19, 145: David Finch/www.judophotos.com
Page 20: AFP/Touchline Photo
Pages 33, 56: Getty Images/Touchline Photo
Page 39: Bohemian Nomad Picturemakers/Corbis
Page 49: AFP/Touchline Photo
Page 63: Richard Bailey/Corbis
Page 67: Digital Source

Disclaimer

Judo involves training in techniques that can cause serious, even life-threatening, injury. Although the author and publisher have made every effort to ensure that the information in this book is accurate, they accept no liability for loss, accident, injury or other damages sustained by anyone using this book. To ensure the safety of you and your training partners, the techniques described in this book must only be practiced under the direct supervision of a qualified black belt judo instructor.

"Books to Span the East and West"

Tuttle Publishing was founded in 1832 in the small New England town of Rutland, Vermont [USA]. Our core values remain as strong today as they were then—to publish best-in-class books which bring people together one page at a time. In 1948, we established a publishing outpost in Japan—and Tuttle is now a leader in publishing English-language books about the arts, languages and cultures of Asia. The world has become a much smaller place today and Asia's economic and cultural influence has grown. Yet the need for meaningful dialogue and information about this diverse region has never been greater. Over the past seven decades, Tuttle has published thousands of books on subjects ranging from martial arts and paper crafts to language learning and literature—and our talented authors, illustrators, designers and photographers have won many prestigious awards. We welcome you to explore the wealth of information available on Asia at **www.tuttlepublishing.com**.

Published by Tuttle Publishing, an imprint of Periplus Editions (HK) Ltd.

www.tuttlepublishing.com

Copyright © 2024, Neil Ohlenkamp

Library of Congress Cataloging-in-Publication Data for this title is in progress

ISBN 978-4-8053-1746-4

27 26 25 24   8 7 6 5 4 3 2 1   2401EP
Printed in China

TUTTLE PUBLISHING® is a registered trademark of Tuttle Publishing, a division of Periplus Editions (HK) Ltd.

Distributed by

North America, Latin America & Europe
Tuttle Publishing
364 Innovation Drive
North Clarendon, VT 05759-9436 U.S.A.
Tel: 1 (802) 773-8930
Fax: 1 (802) 773-6993
info@tuttlepublishing.com
www.tuttlepublishing.com

Japan
Tuttle Publishing
Yaekari Building, 3rd Floor
5-4-12 Osaki
Shinagawa-ku
Tokyo 141 0032
Tel: (81) 3 5437-0171
Fax: (81) 3 5437-0755
sales@tuttle.co.jp
www.tuttle.co.jp

Asia Pacific
Berkeley Books Pte. Ltd.
3 Kallang Sector #04-01
Singapore 349278
Tel: (65) 6741-2178
Fax: (65) 6741-2179
inquiries@periplus.com.sg
www.tuttlepublishing.com